# "Nation" and "State" in Europe

*Anthropological Perspectives*

# "Nation" and "State" in Europe

## Anthropological Perspectives

Edited by R. D. GRILLO

University of Sussex

1980

ACADEMIC PRESS

A Subsidiary of Harcourt Brace Jovanovich, Publishers
London  New York  Toronto  Sydney  San Francisco

ACADEMIC PRESS INC. (LONDON) LTD.
24/28 Oval Road,
London NW1


*United States Edition published by*
ACADEMIC PRESS INC.
111 Fifth Avenue
New York, New York 10003

*British Library Cataloguing in Publication Data*
'Nation' and 'state' in Europe.
  1. Minorities — Europe — Congresses
  2. Ethnology — Europe — Congresses
  3. Europe — Social conditions — Congresses
  4. Europe — Politics and government — 1945 —
Congresses
  I. Grillo R D
301.45'1'094     D1056     80-49766

ISBN 0-12-303060-9

PRINTED IN GREAT BRITAIN BY
T. J. PRESS (PADSTOW) LTD., PADSTOW, CORNWALL

# Contributors

L. F. Baric, Department of Sociological and Political Studies, University of Salford, Salford M5 4WT

Reginald Byron, Department of Social Anthropology, The Queen's University of Belfast, Belfast BT7 1NN

R. D. Grillo, School of African and Asian Studies, University of Sussex, Falmer, Brighton BN1 9QN

Marianne Heiberg, 5 Wilmington House, Highbury Crescent, London N. 5

Rosemary Lumb, Highland and Islands Development Board, Bridge House, 27 Bank Street, Inverness IV1 1QR

Şerif Mardin, Faculty of Administrative Sciences, Bogaziçi University, P.K. 2 Bebek, Istanbul, Turkey

Leonard Mars, Department of Sociology and Anthropology, University College, Swansea SA2 8PP

Jeff Pratt, School of African and Asian Studies, University of Sussex, Falmer, Brighton BN1 1QN

Amalia Signorelli, via Cassia 859, 00189 Rome, Italy

Robert Wade, Institute of Development Studies, University of Sussex, Falmer, Brighton BN1 9QN

# *Preface*

This collection is based on the proceedings of a seminar sponsored by the Social Anthropology Committee of the Social Science Research Council. In 1975-76 the Committee consulted anthropologists in the UK about future research needs in the discipline, and later took up the suggestion that the SSRC itself should initiate meetings which would bring together scholars from Britain and abroad to discuss specialized fields of research. The "Seminar group on anthropological research in industrial societies with particular reference to Western Europe" (the "European" seminar) was one result.

At eight meetings between September 1977 and January 1980 this group, involving 15-20 regular participants and occasional visitors, discussed some 50 papers by anthropologists and others actively engaged in European research. The first meeting planned a programme of seminars each devoted to a major theme: "Identities and boundaries", "State institutions and local communities", "Centre-periphery", "Occupational cultures", "Ideologies and social movements", "Dominant languages", and "The social context of research". The first three generated the papers which form the present collection. A second, provisionally entitled "Ideology, language and power in Europe", is also in preparation.

The "Introduction" to this volume draws extensively on discussions which took place at the seminars. However, although there was much agreement among us there was in no sense a collective view. The responsibility for what is said must rest with the author.

# Contents

# 1

# *Introduction*

*R. D. GRILLO*

"Only by moving grandly on the macroscopic level can we satisfy our intellectual and human curiosities. But only by moving minutely on the molecular level can our observations and explanations be adequately connected. So, if we would have our cake and eat it too, we must shuttle between macroscopic and molecular levels in instituting the problem *and* in explaining it" (Mills, 1963:563).

This book touches on a number of themes in the study of "complex" societies, mainly in the context of contemporary Europe. Specifically it is about "centres" in both a topographical and metaphorical sense, or rather that "centralization" which operating along various axes and at many different levels has long characterized the cultural, political and economic framework within which social relationships in Europe are enacted. Three facets of this centralization interest us: the emergence of supra-local identities and cultures (the "nation"); the rise of powerful and authoritative institutions within the public domain (the "state"), and the development of particular ways of organizing production and consumption (the "economy").

We tentatively explore the contribution from the perspective of social anthropology to the understanding of these three relatively autonomous but interdependent phenomena. Our argument is roughly as follows. The processes associated with the growth and spread of the institutions of the "nation-state", and perhaps its supra-national successor, and those which generate the form of economic organization at national and international levels, sometimes appear monolithic and inexorable. Anthropological research, with its emphasis on the local and specific, suggests that the impact of these processes, and the response they generate, is highly varied. We are therefore confronted by three related questions: How and why does such variation occur? What does this tell us about the relation between part and whole in complex systems? And how may we attack the problem of what are usually conceptualized as "levels" within such systems?

We do not offer definitive solutions to these and other questions. The papers presented to the "European" seminar were intended to stimulate speculation about areas of inquiry that were and are underdeveloped, at least in anthropology, and that intention remains. Moreover, the intrinsic complexity of "nation" and "state" as concepts and social realities, and the fact that their study by anthropologists takes us far beyond what used to be considered our terrain, demands modesty.

This has two implications. First, we must accept that lesson long since learned by those working in the Third World where multi-disciplinary research is normal (see Geertz 1975:327). Cole (1977:368) has charted a similar trend in recent anthropological research in Europe, and we must strengthen it. This does not mean we agree completely with Wallerstein that "when one studies a social system, the classical lines of division within the social sciences are meaningless" (1974:11). There is, we believe, an "anthropological" perspective which illuminates what others say.

The second implication is that we must be thoroughly familiar with their work. The principle of "naivety" towards other disciplines advocated by Gluckman (1964:212ff) still has its adherents, and not only in anthropology. The author of a recent book on the modern state remarks: "I have no doubt that sociologists . . . could benefit from exploring the contributions of other disciplines . . . I myself have made no effort to draw on (them). I find anthropology boring. I do not understand economics" (Poggi 1978:xii-xiii). Ideally our own studies would be set against the mass of scholarly and non-scholarly writing, thought and evidence which our subject matter has generated. This ideal is scarcely attainable in an Introduction such as this. We can, however, try provisionally to place our findings in the context of recent major work on "nation" and "state" in Europe, and to sketch, for anthropology and for anthropologists, the outlines of the intellectual environment within which we are obliged to operate.

## Social Anthropology in Europe

The programme of the "European" seminar grew from an assessment of anthropological research in Europe in the mid-seventies. A number of recent publications (Boissevain and Friedl, 1975; Davis, 1977; Leyton, 1977; and Boissevain, 1979 — originally presented to us) provided our starting point. Cole's equally valuable guide (1977) was not then available.

During the last twenty years the anthropology of Europe has to a marked degree exhibited the discipline's propensity for creating boundaries within which fields of research become "traditions". In the geographical area of the continent and its off-shore islands there emerged several regionally based traditions which barely, if ever, recognized each other's existence: in North-West Europe, for example, with separate foci in Ireland and Britain, in Northern Scandinavia, and above all in the Mediterranean, which for some anthropologists has come to mean "Europe". What Cole (1977:351) calls the "Anglophone Anthropology" of Europe has been largely concerned with that region.

Boundaries have their value, however, and each tradition has explored certain lines of inquiry with great confidence: consider, for example, the wealth of material on ethnicity in Britain, or the honour–shame–patronage–godparenthood complex in the Mediterranean. Great advances have been made, as Davis's excellent summary of Mediterranean research shows. But can we break down these and other existing boundaries (for example that between "urban" and "rural"), and find common ground where we may talk of a "European", as opposed to a "Mediterranean" or "Irish" anthropology? Does "Europe" constitute a meaningful object of social investigation?

Our answer to that question is an equivocal "Yes". First, all European countries are, and have long been, part of a single economic, political and social field in much the same way as have the societies of the Mediterranean (Davis, 1977:18; Boissevain, 1979:83; Boissevain and Friedl, 1975:11; Cole, 1977:367, 372). This is insufficient, however. To define an area of inquiry in that way obliges us to take full account of those forces which structure the field.

Anthropological research in the Mediterranean and elsewhere in Europe has often turned its back on precisely those issues on which a "European" anthropology might be construed.

Davis (1977:5-10) and Leyton (1977) writing independently about the Mediterranean and Ireland produce similar lists of what both term the "failures" of anthropology in their respective areas: the paucity of research outside the village or small town, on the links between town and country, on the relation between local and national in the field of politics or religion, and so on. For example, a reader of Davis's excellent book might be forgiven for not realizing that in each country on the Northern littoral of the Mediterranean, Catholicism is a major force; that each of these countries experienced lengthy periods of fascist rule; that parties of the left enjoy substantial if often clandestine support; that there are major urban and industrial centres of great power; that within each country there are regions of diverse cultural and linguistic composition which have undergone an, at times, painful incorporation within a nation-state; that between regions there are marked inequalities of power and wealth; and that within the Mediterranean the Northern and Southern shores were long bound by a colonial relationship (cf. Cole, 1977:32).

These "failures", which are also rehearsed by Boissevain (1979) and Cole (1977), are more than "gaps in the ethnography". They stem from a major weakness in our orientation towards the local, small-scale manifestations of culture, society and economy, and follow from the role that anthropology has adopted in the division of labour in the social sciences. Anthropological research has located itself among either "Peasant communities" or "Immigrants" (at B2 and A3 in Figure, p. 16) and tended to treat both in isolation from the broader framework of which they are part, and which, in a sense, defines them (cf. Schneider and Schneider, 1976:6).

This, of course, is to exaggerate. Most Mediterranean monographs, to say nothing of research on ethnicity in Britain or Scandinavia, refer to this framework. And Cole (1977:32) is right to point to the work of Davis himself (1973), Blok (1974), and the Schneiders (1976) — to which add Boissevain and Friedl (1975), Brandes (1975), Cutileiro (1971), and Loizos (1975) — as examples of research which attempt to go "beyond the community". By the mid-seventies, it could be argued, the basis for an anthropology of "Europe" was already emerging.

By collating the "failures" of European anthropology we established a positive programme of study which examined certain large-scale processes in evidence in most European countries, North and South, West and East. It is these common processes, which Boissevain and

Friedl list as "state formation, national integration, industrialization, urbanization, bureaucratization, class conflict, and commercialization" (1975:11), that shape the European experience and provide the framework through which a set of "real" societies constitute a single field.

If we define "Europe" as an object of inquiry in these two senses, we do so with four reservations. First, in dissolving one set of boundaries we create another. "Europe" itself forms part of a wider field, and the processes we discuss are obviously not confined to Europe. They are products of what Wallerstein calls a "world-system" comprising a certain type of economy and polity (though they may also be typical of all "modern" societies, capitalist and non-capitalist). Wallerstein's argument is that this world-system emerged in Europe (cf. Tilly 1975:601) whence the institutional form was exported (Rokkan 1970:47). Is there anything uniquely "European" about this system in Europe?

Secondly, continent-wide macro-processes only in part define our object. For if a weakness of anthropology is its emphasis on the micro, which leads it away from the large picture (Shils, 1963:23), it is also a source of strength. Davis puts it this way: "There is a heady intoxicating elixir held out to us by the macro-men . . . the state apparatus, the higher levels of segmentation, consists not simply of depersonalized macro-processes, but of people interacting . . . to replace our current treatment of the state . . . with macro-processes . . . would be to substitute one mystification for another" (1975:49). Our own strategy must be to seek those relationships which are "total" in Mauss's sense, whose ramifications oblige us to "shuttle between macroscopic and molecular levels" (Mills, 1963).

Thirdly, large-scale processes and institutions do not necessarily define the framework of social action at all levels, and even when this happens, they need not determine the content of action or the course that it takes. So then, fourthly, the uniformity of macro-processes is of less interest that their manifestation in particular situations. The varied forms of the outcome of their encounter with the "local", the relationship *between* macro and micro, part and whole, are among the central problems for an anthropology of complex societies.

## On "Nations", "States", and "Nation-states"

"La patrie est un élément humain, sentimental, alors que c'est sur des éléments d'action, d'autorité, de responsabilité qu'on peut construire l'Europe. Quels éléments? Eh bien, les Etats." (Charles de Gaulle, 1970:407).[1]

The macro-processes considered in this volume are to do with the formation of "nation" and "state" and their conjunction in the "nation-state". The two are readily distinguished. "A state is a legal and political organization . . . A nation is a community of people" (Seton-Watson, 1977:1). Some such distinction is necessary. There are, after all, many states which are not nations, and vice versa. Some writers, while recognizing this confound matters by using "nation" to refer to what is here termed the "nation-state". Thus, Marcel Mauss, writing in 1920, defined a "nation" as "une société matériellement et moralement intégrée, à pouvoir central stable, permanent, à frontières déterminées, à relative unité morale, mentale et culturelle des habitants qui adhèrent consciemment à l'Etat et à ses lois" (1969: 584). More recently Fishman (1972:5) has employed the term in a similar sense. Mauss's usage begs many questions concerning the emergence of such entities, and what Poulantzas (1978:105) calls the "peculiar relationship" *between* nation and state.

Certainly during the last two centuries nation- and state-building have gone hand in hand. It is widely agreed, however, that "nation-states", "nations" in Mauss's sense, or at any rate "nationalism" (cf. Lafont, 1968:69), were the product of the late eighteenth century, of the Enlightenment and the French Revolution (Finer, 1975:89; Gordon, 1978:15; Kedourie, 1960:9; Kohn, 1944:3, 10; Seton-Watson, 1977:6; Smith, 1979:4). There were states, and in a sense nations, in Europe long before, but not nation-states. Braudel (1973:657), referring to the Mediterranean in the fifteenth century and the rise of the territorial state as rival to the city-state, deliberately avoids the term. In introducing an important collection Tilly notes that he and his collaborators had intended to "analyse state-making and the formation of nations interdependently" (1975:6), but their material on the eighteenth century and earlier forced them to concentrate on state rather than nation. Strayer who calls England in the fifteenth century a nation-state (1963:24) is one of the few to apply the term in the context of early modern Europe. Perhaps England was a special case, and more typical was France whose structure in 1789 has been described thus: "Autour de l'ethnie proprement française . . . un ensemble de nations ou de lambeaux de nations annexés par la conquête militaire ou la ruse diplomatique" (Lafont, 1968:151).

Confusion arises from what Lafont (1968:35 calls a "dichotomie fondamentale" in the word "nation". His contrast of *nation ethnique* (or *nation "biologique"*) with *nation politique* (or *nation des citoyens*) is similar to one made by Smith (1979:167) between nation as a " 'natural' unit in history" and as a "political goal or ideal". Smith argues that the "ethnic nation" is an "ancient historical and cultural entity", but nation as the "sole basis for politics and government" (Smith, 1979) is a modern phenomenon. Macartney's distinction between "personal" and "political" nationality (1934:13 fl.), which he saw as representing two great traditions which historically characterized Eastern and Western Europe, is again similar.

These distinctions are straightforward enough. They are between "ethnicity", and "ethnicity politicized" through the medium of government to create the nation-state (cf. Fishman, 1972:24 fl.). There is, however, a further "dichotomy" in the words "ethnicity" and "nation" which may refer both to a sense of common identity and the possession of common attributes, usually of culture and language. In either case, the point is the connection of ethnicity to polity.

A number of themes run through discussions of this connection. The first is the way in which the state is articulated through nation, and vice versa. Contemporary European nation-states have evolved through two processes which, says Fishman (1972:28) may be thought of as "contrasted transformations of each other". These processes, which are mentioned by writers as diverse as Cohen (1978:76), Lafont (1968:35), Macartney (1934:13), Poulantzas (1978:95) and Strayer (1963:23), involve on the one hand states which attempt to construct nations from what might be a highly heterogeneous collection of citizens, and on the other "nations" which demand, and in some cases obtain, an autonomous state. I refer to these as the "politicization of ethnicity" (i.e. nation ⟶ state) and the "ethnicization of the polity" (state ⟶ nation).

Almost all European countries have experienced these processes in various ways and at different times. Most authorities would agree with Wallerstein, however, that "the creation of strong states within a world-system was a historical prerequisite to the rise of nationalism both within strong states and in the periphery" (1974:145). That is, polity preceded ethnicity. France is usually offered as the classic illustration of this where, following the Revolution, ethnicization of the polity became conscious policy in the Jacobinist tradition. The question whether such ethnicization occurred earlier in France or elsewhere (e.g. England), albeit in a less conscious fashion, must be left to one side.

Ethnicization involves the construction and transmission of a strong sense of common identity, a central problem for several papers in this collection, and the spread of common cultural forms, including language, disseminated through the institutions of the state. Mauss (1969:591), Poulantzas (1978:58), Smith (1979:171), Tarrow (1977: 47 fl.), and Tilly (1975:78-79) have each commented on this latter process which is well documented for countries such as France (Gordon, 1978:30–31, 97; Lafont, 1968; Weber, 1976). Surprisingly, it is not something which has attracted much anthropological attention, except perhaps in immigrant ethnic studies, though some contributors to Boissevain and Friedl (1975) (e.g. Snell and Snell) allude to it.

Why ethnicization, or "national integration" as some call it, occurred in Europe is an intriguing question, and one not easy to answer if posed in the manner of Poulantzas: "Why and how do territory, historical tradition and language chart by means of the State the new configuration that is the modern nation?" (1978:97). Miliband (1973:185), Tilly (1975:78–79), Wallerstein (1974:348) and Poulantzas himself (1978:58, 96–97) reply by stressing the function of such integration for the economic and political order. Their assumption is that nations are constructed and not "natural" entities. They clothe, and enclose, an existing or developing political and economic framework.

This assumption, which I believe partly correct, would seem to make explanation of the "politicization of ethnicity" more difficult than expected. For are not the identities thus politicized "primary" or "basic", "ancient" and "primordial" (cf. Geertz, 1975:263)? The idea that culture, language and race define "natural" or "historic" groups is certainly a premise of nationalist ideology, as is the proposition that they have the right of self-determination (see Kedourie, 1960:58, 68). Our attitude towards this question is important. It has a bearing on our understanding of what generates "autonomist" movements, as we shall see.

There are in Europe few, if any, states where ethnicization is complete, as Stephens (1976) exhaustive accounting of extant minority language groups shows. Even those where an apparently homogeneous nation has achieved autonomy are essentially what Lafont calls "nations secondaires" (1968:66–67) and Strayer "mosaic states" (1963:23). Besides indigenous differences of an ethnic or cultural kind, based on regional differentiation or long-established residence, the operation of the labour market has in the last century introduced substantial numbers of ethnic immigrants into many countries, adding a new dimension to existing heterogeneity.

How the mosaic is put together, the "integration" whether of immigrant minorities or of constituent territorial elements, has long been of interest to anthropologists and others. The development of "national" identities and cultures has often meant the penetration of a territory and the absorption of its people in forms emanating from one powerful region or group. Recently, the territorial mosaic in Europe has been analysed as a set of relationships between "centres" (or "cores") and "peripheries" (Boissevain, 1979; Cole, 1977:368; Rokkan, 1970, 1975; Schneider and Schneider, 1976; Seers *et al.*, 1979; Tarrow, 1977). In geographical terms, this kind of centralization has been located on three levels: within a global system embracing Europe and other parts of the world (Wallerstein's "world-system"); within Europe, between strong states or supra-national regions and weaker ones; and within states, between their component regions. Several papers in this volume take up this aspect of centralization, though Mardin follows Shils in employing "centre" and "periphery" in a metaphorical sense where "centre" stands for "central values" (Shils, 1961; cf. Mardin, 1972).

Whether dealing with values or territory, identity, culture, government or economy, we are discussing a set of related processes which provide, sometimes in conjunction, sometimes in opposition, central pivots around which society, potentially at all levels, may be ordered. These processes have characterized Europe for the last two hundred years or more, and continue to define the framework within which our own part research must be located. One approach to their study is that which sees such processes as both shaping and being shaped by salient social identities. Operating at many different levels where they create "new" identities or give a novel twist to existing ones, they constitute the conditions under which the concepts of "Us" and the opposition between "Us" and "Them" are formed.

## "Us" and "Them": Identity and Boundary

Nation-states are founded on the widely accepted premise that "nationality" is a significant identity. Both states which seek to become nations, and nations which seek to mobilize their people in the demand for a state, are engaged in creating and diffusing an identity, and establishing and maintaining a boundary between "Us" and "Them". How such identities are articulated is an important question. Here we are concerned mainly with the ideology and symbolism of national identities, with those aspects which Seton-Watson dismisses as "rhetoric" (1977:445), but which seem essential for the inculcation of a sense of nation at all levels, even if, perhaps especially if, such identities serve as an "ideological mask" (Wallerstein, 1974:348).

In modern Europe "nation" has come to refer to communities of a

specific kind. Whatever the word *natio* meant in an earlier period (see
Kedourie, 1960:14–15; Mauss, 1969:573–574; Macartney, 1934: 62;
Seton-Watson, 1977:8; Smith, 1979:167) we are concerned with its
modern sense, even in those papers which have a certain historical
depth. Our approach places the discussion of national identity in the
broader context of "difference" and its expression (cf. Kohn, 1944:
10–13). "Difference" is to be distinguished from "differentiation"
(Wallman, 1978:201). In Europe, as everywhere, there are constantly
shifting patterns of social, cultural and economic differentiation which
may or may not be translated into the actor's experience of significant
differences.

These are differences which give rise to the sense of "Us" and
"Them", which say who "We" are. There is always a multiplicity of
potential differentiae which might bear this load and convey this sense.
Some are sign-like in that they have a plausible relationship with the
"reality" of who we are or what we do. Others are more obviously
constructed. National identities are both.

In Europe the bases for difference are not extensive. Place,
occupation, class, power, gender, age, religion, ideology, culture,
language, race and nation seem the most important (cf. Geertz, 1975:
261–263). They are kaleidoscopic in that two or more may appear to
coincide, or one may become central with others providing support,
directly or indirectly through secondary symbolic elaboration. Here we
take nation as the central or pivotal referent, from which perspective
the rest, appearing in conjunction, or in opposition, constitute the
" 'ethnographic material' out of which under certain circumstances a
nationality may arise" (Kohn, 1944:13; cf. Krejci, 1978:126;
Macartney, 1934:7; Wallerstein, 1974:353). The phrase "ethnographic
material" is a potent one for anthropologists. Identities such as "Our
nation" are constructed, perhaps by "une sorte de bricolage intellectuel"
(Lévi-Strauss, 1962:26) from a relatively closed universe of such
elements which comprise the European repertoire.

It may be objected that this suggests that national identities are
entirely fabricated, whereas they reflect an underlying ethnic, cultural
or linguistic "reality". In the first place, our concern is with their
employment as salient markers of difference. It was not inevitable that
those elements would achieve that status. Moreover, ethnic, cultural
and linguistic differentiation is itself the result of a process which has to
be understood. This is not to deny that, once made salient, national
identity and its component elements attain a kind of autonomous
"reality" and force of their own.

Viewing nationality as a constructed salient difference leads us to see
that "Our nation" is a stage in the social production and transmission

of the concept of one kind of "Us", when "We-potential" has become "We-actual". It also makes clear that the identity, and the implied boundary between "Us" and "Them", must vary in intensity, and probably content, situationally and historically.

In traditional anthropology the emergence of identity was never seriously considered. Within a synchronic frame of reference, such as was usually employed, the coming-into-being and historic variation of identity cannot constitute a problem. For those working in Europe such variation is problematic simply because history, the record of past events, tells us so. But it is *in* history, the flow of past events, that emergence and variation appear, and only *through* history can we understand them. This is rather more than what Davis calls "history (as) a kind of social change" (1977:246). In any event, it demands that the anthropologist must become in a sense an historian as the papers by Baric, Heiberg, Pratt and Vermeulen all illustrate.

History is not used by the analyst alone, however. Lévi-Strauss's remark about "hot" societies which "interiorise history . . . and turn it into the motive power of their development" (Charbonnier, 1969:39) forces us to examine the constant interpretation and re-interpretation of history called to the aid of "Our" identity. For example, over the last two and a half millennia there have been many "centres" in Europe, and many "peripheries". There is a legacy which may be, and often is, exploited to sustain the present, as in the ideology and symbolism of Mussolini's Italy (*Mare Nostrum*, etc.) or in modern Hellenism. This mythologizing of history is a recurrent feature of national identity construction which bedevils the entire discussion of supposed national roots when these are located in some "historic" ethnic past.

Historians themselves, professional and amateur, and other intellectuals including, let it be said, anthropologists, have played a part in the elaboration and diffusion of such myth history, and in the reconstruction, even creation, of languages and cultures said to be "Ours". Although much has been written about such intellectuals (e.g. Dumont, 1979; Kedourie, 1960; Kohn, 1946, 1967; Macartney, 1934; Smith, 1976:16–25; Smith, 1979; Snyder, 1964) attention has been focussed mainly on their roles as formulators of the ideological and philosophical bases of nationalism, and their political function at the highest levels. How their ideas become part of the general discourse of those to whom they would seem directed — the bulk of ordinary people said to comprise "Our nation" — is less well documented. It is a matter on which anthropologists should have something to say, given their preoccupation with the local and popular. The papers by Baric and Heiberg are implicitly concerned with this.

An historical perspective emphasises the variable nature of both signified and signifier — "Our" identity and its mode of expression. An intriguing example is what we called "switching" of the kind described by Heiberg, here and elsewhere, in her account of the Basques. At one time to be "Basque" is to be conservative, in a political sense; at another, or for others, it is to be socialist and revolutionary. This is not a simple case of old identities in new clothing, or new identities in a "time-honoured disguise", as Marx (1968:96) called it, but a complex interweaving of the two. A study of Irish nationalism would provide an illuminating comparison.

Such switching is never, of course, arbitrary. In the case of the Basques (and perhaps the Irish) it must at least partly reflect the social and economic position of the groups and individuals whose version of "Our" identity holds sway. There is another reason. Lévi-Strauss says of the *bricoleur's* use of materials that "ces possibilités demeurent toujours limitées par l'histoire particulière de chaque pièce" (1962: 28–9). Perhaps not fortuitously one recalls Marx: "Men make their own history, but they do not make it just as they please . . . The tradition of all the dead generations weighs like a nightmare on the brain of the living" (1968:96).

An example of this might be when in mid-twentieth century Europe "Our" identity is expressed in terms of race rather than culture or language. The symbolic and behavioural implications are more profound not least because the element "race" is preconstrained by its history. A shift from, say, culture to race increases the temperature as it were and represents, or may be represented as, a highly charged step.

This has implications for our understanding of the elements which are adduced in support of "nation", especially those which provide secondary elaboration. Consider, for example, the symbolic construction which may be placed on various ways of defining the right to belong. Pitt-Rivers has observed the importance in different parts of Europe of *ius sanguinis* and *ius soli* as contrasting modes of jural incorporation which define a community (Pitt-Rivers, 1954:30; cf. Macartney, 1934:29, 32). The Basque evidence discussed by Heiberg indicates we should add right by belief and by act.

This suggests important ways in which the construction of national identity varies from one cultural group or region to another. In Europe, with what variation is not clear, we sometimes find the idiom of kinship employed as a secondary elaboration (e.g. the Irish Republican Brotherhood). And what of the elements which make up different representations of "Our" or "Their" personalities? Does this imply a specifically French, or German, or Italian repertoire and style of construction?

For instance, Pratt shows how the symbol of the walled city was employed as a campaign device by Italian Christian Democrats, and comments: "This enduring representation of the contrast between . . . insider and outsiders . . . is transposed to the national level" (this Volume, p. 41). How might such cultural variation be reflected in the utterances of a Mazzini, or a Michelet or a Fichte (cf. Dumont, 1979)?

Pratt's material on the use of the organic analogy to present a sense of "Us" which masks or places a certain construction on "Our" internal differentiation provides a further example from the Italian repertoire, and raises another question. Such symbolic usage expresses the idea that "Our" bonds are primary and natural. Under what circumstances are such "natural" symbols employed? Is it a matter of cultural variation, or are they more widely favoured, either when identities and boundaries are highly charged, or when an added charge is needed? Nature reinforces culture and culturally significant differences in complex ways. There is never a simple opposition between "We" = "Culture"/"They" = "Nature". A contrast within nature itself may be utilized, as when "We" are of one blood, but "They" are beasts.

It must never be forgotten that identity construction is a political process. There are many groups in Europe who fall short of saying "We" are, or should be, a nation. Krejci (1978:136) lists 69 European ethnic groups of which, in 1976, 24 had states. In many other cases, but by no means all, there was a history of demands for a state, or integration with states which represented their national identities. What mechanisms are at work here? Baric's paper perhaps shows that local Slovene cultural leaders in Italy have an interest in maintaining Slovene identity at a moderate level of intensity. Too little, and their *raison d'être* disappears, too much and the political context becomes too difficult.

This example illustrates something else. The societies we study are highly differentiated with marked divergences of interest unequally integrated in systems of power. Definitions of "Us" reflect this, as a comparison of the view of Slovene identity held by politically conscious elite groups with that held by the population at large might show. Complexities of this kind in local situations lead us to view with suspicion accounts concerned with the broadest perspective which is often that of the activists at the centre. "We" utterances must be treated as partial statements of claims rather as descriptions of a reality which prevails at all levels.

Kedourie reports an episode which delights anthropologists who favour what Geertz calls "spiteful ethnography" (1975:330). Before World War I, a linguistic inquiry was instituted to decide the fate of Epirus. "The partisans of Greece visited the villages in dispute and obtained answers in Greek; in the same villages the partisans of Albania obtained answers in Albanian; and occasionally . . . a villager would answer in Albanian, 'I am Greek' " (Kedourie, 1960:124). Vermeulen's account (1978) of nearby Macedonia in roughly the same period shows that choice of national identity on the part of villagers has to be understood as much in terms of local as of supra-local interests. What are the consequences for their eventual incorporation in a system of nation-states in which the salient differences between "Us" and "Them" are articulated through national identities which they might be supposed to have chosen for other reasons?

"Our" incorporation within an identity, and the establishment and protection of a boundary between "Us" and "Them" are political activities involving many divergent interests which may have different meaning at various levels of social organization. They also entail the elaboration of an ideological and symbolic system through which the concept of "Us" is projected in such a way that it becomes part of the predominant mode of discourse, an aspect of everyone's everyday experience. At one level, it might appear that European nation-states achieved that kind of homogeneity, perhaps to a surprising degree. At the same time, countervailing identities and boundaries continued under certain circumstances to be maintained or even strengthened, sometimes as a result of the operation of the very mechanisms by which incorporation was attempted.

## *"Us" and "Them": Centre and Periphery*

Nation-building occurred within an existing, if changing, framework of cultural, social and economic differentiation. It also created new kinds of differentiation, and difference, both between and within nation-states. Writing of eighteenth century France and England, Macartney remarks: "The national kingdoms crystallized outwards, by slow process of accumulation from central nuclei" (1934:44). The only cultural minorities to survive were "on the periphery, in extreme and inhospitable corners of the land . . . peasants and mountaineers" (Macartney, 1934). Lafont's description of France cited earlier suggests that Macartney exaggerated the extent of national integration, at least by the eighteenth century, and Weber (1976) appears to argue that France did not become "One and Indivisible" until at least 1914. Even when the dominant central culture successfully penetrated the distant parts of the state's territory, it did not follow that there was integration on the basis of equality.

There have always been centres and peripheries in Europe (cf. Rokkan, 1975), but they have not always been the same, and their relationship has not always taken the same form. This is sometimes forgotten in contemporary discussions of centre–periphery which have tended to analyse their relationship almost exclusively through the concept of "dependency", drawing on work in Latin America and Africa and applying a model derived from the study of relations between Europe (and America) and the Third World. Similarly, "dependent" regions are sometimes referred to as "internal colonies" (see Hechter, 1975), an idea which originated in Gramsci's analysis of the position of Southern Italy.

We are in substantial agreement with Tarrow (1977:ch.1) on the limitations of this perspective. The dependency model specifies only one type of centre–periphery relationship, which in turn is only one way in which the elements of the mosaic may be structured. This is not to deny that the model describes what might be the prevailing mode of incorporation in contemporary Europe. There is undoubtedly an economic heartland (Seers *et al.*, 1979:21). There are economically and politically central places which under some circumstances "create" underdevelopment. There are peripheral regions which are, for example, obliged to exchange migrants for tourists (Seers *et al.*, 1979). The dependency model does have the virtue of forcing us to look closely at the influence of the economic order. Nevertheless its emphasis on the determinant nature of the economic order often leads to analyses which are asocial, acultural, apolitical, and frequently anhistoric.

The economic reductionism is apparent in the discussion of transfer payments between countries and regions. In contemporary Europe that an area (or group) may be defined as peripheral (or marginal) may represent a resource in itself, or offer the possibility of resources. Why should the centre — the economy acting through the state — devote resources to peripheral or marginal groups? One view is that all such transfers are to the ultimate economic advantage of the centre (cf. Poulantzas, 1978:185, 189). Wade's paper on Southern Italy shows the relationship to be much more complex than that. The Gaelic-speaking areas of the West of Ireland provide an intriguing example. They attract a high level of support not least because they contain the few remaining native speakers of the language, and as such symbolize the national heritage.

Our own perspective is undoubtedly influenced by the location of our studies at the periphery (see Figure). Despite other weaknesses, it allows us to see that centre–periphery relations are always multiplex,

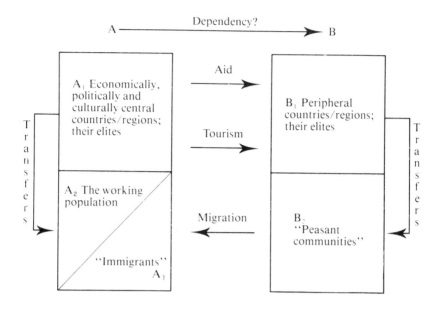

and that a periphery may be orientated towards numerous centres. Rare are the cases where all forms of power (administrative, economic, cultural, linguistic, religious, military, intellectual, educational, ethnic) stem from the same centre and bear with equal, mutually reinforcing, weight on a peripheral region, creating both the conditions for, and the status of "dependency".

The dependency model of centre–periphery relations says everything, and nothing. Even if we allow that a general process of this kind is at work, within countries and between countries, the impact of this process on particular localities may be very different. This emerges from the papers by Byron, Vermeulen and Wade, and in Tarrow's comparison of France and Italy where forces from the centre produce "divergent effects on the periphery" (Tarrow, 1977:7).

It is also an obvious error to assume that the status of a peripheral region has always been of a "dependent" kind. Vermeulen's account (1978) of Macedonia in the late nineteenth century reveals in effect an area in transition between satellite status in the Ottoman *millet* system to what might become "dependency" in a system of modern nation-states. At the time, various centres competed for the allegiance of a poly-ethnic region, presumably for the sake of national integration, providing a resource which local people could utilize. The Schneiders' book on Western Sicily (1976) seems, despite its great historical depth, to over-simplify past relationships in seeking to explain a contemporary "dependency".

Although the mosaic may comprise a centre with peripheries, the relationship takes, and has taken, many different forms. This suggests questions we cannot answer. What accounts for the variation of this form? What kind of conditions are likely to be generated at local levels? What changes, disappears, or survives? In general, what is likely to occur in the incorporation of localities in different kinds of supra-local system? Anthropology is often good at showing what has happened in a particular case, and why it happens. We are poor at developing more general models, except of a very simple kind (see the discussion of "functionary–client" in the next section) which we explore with a check-list showing what has been influential in other instances.

Sometimes we go a little further. For example, the outcome of any interaction between large-scale forces (nation, state, economy) and a locality must depend on the nature of existing bases of economic and political power at the local level, and on the relationship that may be negotiated between local and national elites (Schneider and Schneider, 1976:150). The papers by Baric and Heiberg (Chapters 4 and 3, this Volume) and Vermeulen (1978) provide numerous illustrations.

It will be seen later, in our discussion of the state, that an important problem for us is the explanation of collective action. Under what circumstances does peripheral status generate a collective response on the part of those at the margin? Rokkan has in fact identified as one of four major cleavages within nation-states that between the "central nation-building culture" and the "ethnically, linguistically or religiously distinct subject populations in . . . the peripheries" (1970:102). The examples most frequently cited where centre–periphery has generated a salient cleavage are indeed those in which the collectivity may plausibly organize about an ethnic identity: "We" Basques, Bretons, Corsicans, Irish, Scots, etc. Are, then, peripheral movements likely to be strong when ethnically based, and must regional movements throughout Europe be understood by reference to the regions' peripheral status?

In part, yes. Powerful central cultures, presenting themselves as the nation and acting through the state, try to create homogeneous entities which may in fact order ethnic identity, culture and language hierarchically. This must not be confused with the argument that ethnicity is a natural premise for collective action. It is not because Irish, Bretons or Basques are *natural* groups that they organize about their ethnic identity. Their ethnicity is generated by the system of nation-states in which they find themselves. The nation-states created the rules of the game by making identity, culture and language salient markers of difference. The regional minorities respond in kind. As Poulantzas says: *"Jacobinism* and *separatism* are two aspects of the same phenomenon" (1978:105). Perhaps the ethnicity of immigrant groups should be seen in the same light?

Attempts to impose or evolve national identities, cultures and languages, the operation of the economic order, and the structure and activities of the state all play a part in this, as the Snells' article (1975) on the Sames of Northern Scandinavia shows. And there need not be total subjection, or complete "alienation" as Lafont (1968:154) defines it. If centralization incorporates unequally into the totality, it does so unevenly. The Spanish Basques described by Heiberg are in an economically central, but politically, culturally and linguistically peripheral region (cf. Seton-Watson 1977:58; Smith 1979:160). Deprivation is well known to be relative.

In both past and present the state has had a crucial hand in the incorporative process through which "Our nation" has been built. However, Smith (1979:160 fl.) and Tarrow (1977:16, 27), from different if mutually supporting perspectives, emphasize the role of the state in creating *anti*-national consciousness in peripheries. The impersonality of the bureaucratic machine, technological rationalism, and centralized planning are, according to Smith, three aspects of state organization which "generate new cultural awareness and . . . political resentment" (Smith, 1979:173). This view of the state's role in nation-building meshes with our own which is explored in the next Section.

## "Us" and "Them": States and Clients

Our eventual purpose is to carry forward the discussion of the emergence of salient social differences by examining the role of the state in contemporary national structures. The first, and major, task is, however, to develop a perspective for that purpose. Space will not allow consideration of one vital aspect of the state's role — its organization of institutions through which national cultures are transmitted.

Poggi (1978:ix), Miliband (1973:4) and Tilly (1975:617) complain that the state is neglected by social scientists despite our increasing awareness of what Poggi calls "the basic trend . . . of the modern state

— the gathering unto it of ever more formidable faculties and facilities of rule" (1978:10). The extensive writing of Poulantzas (1975, 1976, 1978) and others in France, and recent work in Britain and elsewhere (e.g. Daedalus, 1979; Hayward and Berki, 1979; Dyson, 1980) suggest, however, that the state is now very much on the agenda.

So far the anthropological contribution has been meagre, and Rew exaggerates only mildly when saying "there is very little theoretical or empirical work which could be termed 'the social anthropology of bureaucracy and the contemporary state' " (1977:6). Centralized systems of traditional government have certainly provided the staple of political anthropology. Such studies (and many examples might be cited) focus on the pivotal authority (king, paramount chief), his family, retinue, rituals, landholding, administrative staffs and so on. There has recently been a resurgence of interest in the "origins" of such systems (e.g. Claessen and Skalnik, 1978; Cohen and Service, 1978). This work offers insights for the historian of feudal Europe or the age of Absolutism (cf. Geertz, 1975:339; Tilly, 1975:621-2), and has its relevance for the study of the contemporary state. Historical studies of state-building in Europe also employ perspectives which anthropologists can develop, as Blok's use of the work of Norbert Elias testifies, and certain shared concerns of historians, and anthropologists of traditional states, in fact provide our own starting point.

State formation, says Bayley, involves a "process of penetration of a territory by a coherent set of institutions along . . . several dimensions" (1975:362). The relevant institutions are listed by Miliband as government and administration at all levels, forces of law and order, and systems of public representation. These "make up 'the state', and (their) interrelationship shapes the form of the state system" (Miliband, 1973:50). In the early modern period in Europe, and perhaps elsewhere in traditional systems, these institutions were closely tied to what Finer calls the "extraction–coercion cycle". This cycle, he says, lay at the heart of the evolution of Brandenberg-Prussia in the eighteenth century: "A set of officials to control the logistics of the expanding army . . . and to extract revenue for it, comingled to form a dense, hard-working excessively regulated and regulating bureaucracy; and this formed the spinal column of a *state*" (Finer, 1975:136).

Such states, as they grew in the nineteenth century, provided the institutional apparatus around which the nation-state was formed and which in turn inspired the demands of nations. The form this process took in different European countries is of obvious importance for anthropologists concerned with the histories of their communities. In contemporary Europe, however, the state deals with much more than extraction and coercion. Of equal if not greater significance is the hitherto increasing scale of state intervention in the economic and social order (Elder, 1979; 58 fl., Miliband, 1973:10). To the "extraction–coercion cycle" must be added "intervention" and "distribution". The reasons for this development cannot be considered here (see Hayward and Berki, 1979:225; Causer, 1978; Miliband, 1973; Poulantzas, 1978). The consequences are apparent.

To a variable degree the state is the vehicle through which a multitude of resources is channelled, including that vast range of transactions called transfer payments. These transactions may be analysed from many angles: as a set of "depersonalized macroprocesses", for example, or as the function of an administrative system with its own internal structure and logic (cf. Crozier 1964, esp. Part Three). Our own perspective, inspired to some extent by the work of Davis (1975), E. Marx (1976) and Rew (1977), is as follows.

The aphorism *"L'Etat, c'est moi"*, whether or not attributable to Louis XIV (see Poggi, 1978:161), epitomizes a key feature of the Absolutist state, as it might of an African kingdom, and provides a pivot for analysis. The aphorism *"L'Etat, c'est l'homme derrière un guichet"* likewise epitomizes a central feature of the modern state whose activities demand a vast army of functionaries at all levels (Bendix, 1964:141). Social relationships with the state are in large part enacted with its functionaries, directly and indirectly. These relationships are of special significance when, as is often the case in the situations we study, they coordinate the distribution of, access to, and decisions about basic resources: jobs, housing, education, welfare, health, the environment, development. Thus at the centre of our analysis is the "functionary–client relationship", which we use as an entry to those aspects of the state's activities which have most bearing on our research.

In the first instance this relationship may be treated as a simple ideal-type with the following properties. It must be seen as a relationship in which neither party can be considered in isolation — just as the concept "patron" makes no sense without a concept of "client". It forms a "node" (Marx n.d.) which offers a starting point for an analysis which must move in a number of directions since it links several fields of relations. It is "total", comprised of a multiplicity of aspects, and embedded in a society-wide system of relations of power. It is enacted within a framework of varied values which reflect and are reflected in the wider culture (cf. Crozier, 1964).

This simple model provides a guide only to analysis, but it is a useful one in that it forces us to "open up" the study of administrative systems and move between various levels and systems of social organization.

The model also suggests how intersocietal comparisons might be incorporated. Davis writes of the Mediterranean that "bureaucracies and administrations vary from society to society (but) not enough work has yet been done by anthropologists to show how these variations affect local communities" (1977:102). This may seem unjust to the many studies of bureaucracy since Weber, but when Davis refers to the effects on local communities we may concur.

By making "functionary–client" analytically central and using it to examine local–state relations we are able to see how effects might vary from one society to another. For example, Pizzorno's contrast (cited in Davis, 1977:102) between Roman Law and Anglo-Saxon-based administrative systems, and Berki's possibly similar distinction between "transcendentalist" and "instrumentalist" conceptions of the relation between "state" and "society" (Hayward and Berki, 1979) reveal differences which have consequences for the relative superordination (and autonomy?) of the state in regard to the citizen, of the functionary over the client.

These and other structural factors shape the likely outcome of the functionary–client relationship. Further examples may be suggested. The state is not a monolithic entity, though it may be perceived as such. There is always, to a variable degree, horizontal and vertical differentiation. The extent of specialization, or the devolution of power, may be vastly different. The very boundary between state and non-state institutions may be vague, as may the definition of the "state" functionary. Within institutions the form of hierarchy varies, as does the status accorded the jobs of the personnel, their social and cultural backgrounds, beliefs and so on. Another kind of example is suggested by Marx's paper (1978) on Israel where the point is the sheer extent of state participation. This implies comparisons of the amount and kind of state involvement, direct and indirect, by ownership, control and intervention, all important variables for understanding the functionary–client relationship and its operation in different parts of Europe.

Bearing these and other factors in mind we concentrate on three related ways in which the functionary–client relationship varies: the degree of "disjunction" between functionaries and clients; the "encapsulation" of the relationship; and the nature of "representation" between the parties.

Davis (1977:76) describes bureaucracy in the Mediterranean as a form of stratification because it is a manifestation of power at the centre. Bureaucracy stratifies in other ways too: the system itself is usually hierarchical; functionaries usually, though not always, have high status jobs; and they often come from backgrounds which differentiate them socially from clients. "Disjunction" is influenced by each of these. In several of our own papers two sources of social disjunction stand out: class, and ethnic or national identity.

In many anthropological studies the functionary is a middle-class, educated, relatively well-paid representative of a dominant group who may well come from the "centre", dealing with clients who are peasants or workers, poorly educated or illiterate, and who are often members of an ethnic or regional minority. Such clients may be defined as "marginal" in other ways where the distribution of resources such as housing, education or health is involved. Often, therefore, the status and "language" (in the broadest sense) of the two parties differ markedly.

It is this disjunction, as much as anything, which underpins the widely reported sense of powerlessness. Loizos (1975:121) records that in Cyprus "the impersonality of civil service norms strikes many villagers as a cause not for security but for anxiety." Disjunction, however, cuts both ways. Clients may be lost in the bureaucratic system, but functionaries may have little knowledge of their clients, or that knowledge may be shaped by ideological, intellectual or cultural suppositions. Both points are illustrated in my paper on social workers in Lyon (cf. Ballard, 1978).

Whether or not knowledge, rather than sheer power, counts, both sides may seek it. Functionaries may well believe they require knowledge to make policy, arrive at decisions, monitor their effectiveness, or simply carry out their daily activities. Our papers provide numerous examples. Signorelli's research was stimulated by policy makers' need for knowledge about the returned migrants she discusses. Such research raises questions about the role of social scientists who find themselves participating in a form of indirect representation through which institutions are informed of clients' "problems".

A high degree of disjunction, coupled with the state's role as extractor, intervener and distributor, provides fertile ground for all manner of third parties: experts, lawyers, brokers, patrons and the like. This leads us to ask about the insulation of the functionary–client relationship from outside pressures from politicians, businessmen, churchmen and other *prominenti*. There are obviously degrees of such "encapsulation", between levels and between systems as a whole. In France, according to Poulantzas (1978:223) "the state bureaucracy has shut itself up in a watertight container almost blocking the access channel formerly open to deputies and political parties", whereas in Italy there has occurred, according to Wheaton (1979:55), a "colonisation of the bureaucracy" by Christian Democratic interests. The contrast between France and Italy leads Tarrow to compare what he terms "Dirigiste" (France) and "Clientelistic" (Italy) state systems (Tarrow, 1977:46, 171-2).

Wade's paper on Southern Italy, and Mars's comments on *protktsia* in Israel illustrate aspects of "clientelistic" systems, and provide a link between our own research and earlier work on patronage in Southern Europe (cf. Blok, 1974:212; Boissevain, 1966; Davis, 1977:ch. 4; Gellner and Waterbury, 1977; Loizos, 1975:115-122; Weingrod, 1967 and many others). Gellner's suggestion (in Gellner and Waterbury, 1977:5) that the distribution of patronage in the Mediterranean may be correlated with the weakness of the state would seem to require modification, unless a high degree of disjunction and encapsulation is taken as an index of the strength (or autonomy) of the administration. In any event, both Gellner's argument, and our own, beg some important questions and suggest the need for further research.

If patronage, as a mode of "representation" (cf. Davis, 1977:128), is one way of bridging disjunction, then systems of "participation" of the kind discussed by Lumb are another. Baric (1968:11) has distinguished between "induced" and "indicative" participation: that which allows institutions to explain their wishes, and that which incorporates in planning, say, perhaps at quite high levels (cf. Hayward in Hayward and Berki, 1979:34–38). Either way it is usually the functionaries who effectively define the limits within which participation occurs.

The varied mix of official and unofficial channels of communication, of direct and indirect modes of representation, which both reflect and are reflected in the form of the state system, have important consequences for links between local communities and the centre, and for the ways in which clients organize their individual or collective response to the state's activities. Because our fieldwork tends to be at the grass roots, where the majority of clients are located, responses to the state on their part are relatively well documented by anthropologists as a number of papers in this collection and in Boissevain and Friedl (1975) attest. Social historians also have much to say. Ardant (1975:167) insists on the importance of taxation as an instigator of one type of response — rebellion — throughout the early period of state formation when, according to Tilly, "most members of the population over which managers of states were trying to extend their control resisted the state-making efforts (often with sword and with pitchfork)" (in Tilly, 1975). Crozier refers to the frequent occasions in France when violence, or the threat of civil disorder, has been employed as a strategy to influence the state "whenever a deprived group has felt unable to make its voice heard through the legal system of action" (1964).

Although *individual* violence as a patterned response through which
attempts are made to influence functionaries is analysed at length by
E. Marx (1976), violent collective action specifically directed against
the state and its functionaries — whether as rebellion or revolution —
has rarely been studied by anthropologists, except where other factors
such as ethnicity seem prominent (but see Blok, 1975). The responses
we document tend to be of three kinds.

The first is a type of accommodative reaction when individuals and
groups broadly accept the framework imposed from without and make
adjustments as best they can: the reorganization of fishing boats in the
Shetlands, described by Byron (Chapter 9, this Volume), provides one
illustration. The second is a more positive response in which individuals
manipulate the framework itself, as when Macedonian farmers and
businessmen exploit a complex array of ethnic opportunities, or when
individual "claimants" mobilize their resources, including those held
by members of their social networks, to obtain access to the things
which functionaries control (cf. Boissevain, 1966; Handelman, 1976;
Marx, 1976; Rew, 1977).

The strategy used by anthropologists to analyse such manipulation is
often employed in their examination of a third type or response,
collective organization. Collective mobilization of the kind described in
Yoon's (1975) account of Provençal wine cooperatives, at a time
(1969–71) when every effort was exerted to restrain violence, is
well-documented by anthropologists studying the field of production.
Mars's paper describes a situation where the producers are employees
of the state (Chapter 8, this Volume). Hitherto we have been less
concerned with collective action in the field of consumption, though
research in Britain (Craig *et al.*, 1979) and in France (Pickvance, 1976)
shows its growing importance. Lumb's paper touches on this (Chapter 7,
this Volume).

Our discussions of collective action about the functionary client
relationship underlined the importance of relative degrees of encapsulation of functionaries: the extent to which they can be "reached" via
institutions formally outside the state system, but perhaps connected to
it — parties, unions, churches, patrons; their responsiveness to public
opinion or the media, when there is access to it; their vulnerability at
points in planning and electoral cycles. We also stressed the size and
nature of the "stake" (financial and symbolic), and the kind of base on
which the collectivity is mobilized.

Although those with the strongest economic base (e.g. the workers of
the Israel Ports Authority) appear to have the most muscle, the
strength of local community organization and identity is equally

important. Ballard's (1978) discussion of "politico-ethnic" bargaining indicates one basis for a strong collective response, and suggests an inherent weakness in the perspective which treats collective action as if it were aggregate behaviour on the part of network-manipulating individuals. This is to omit what is frequently a defining characteristic of collective response, an ideological element.

That, under certain circumstances, the operations and activities of the state may generate a response of a collective kind has an important bearing on our previous discussion. The national process establishes a difference between "Us" and "Them" which signifies the essential unity of "Us" as insiders against "Them" as outsiders. Whether or not the state is seen as a simple reflection of "class" or "economic" forces, or whether it is perceived as having a certain "autonomy", the state has had a significant role in creating the form and diffusing the content of nation. Yet its very mode of organization may reflect and generate cleavages which "nation" cannot mask. Another kind of difference may emerge in which "They" are the powers-that-be, *le pouvoir*. So although in one respect nation and state work in conjunction, in another they are in opposition.

This opposition appears strongest among two social categories whose dependence on the modern state as intervener, distributor, and coercer is greatest, and who are the least well "integrated" in the nation: ethnic immigrants, and the inhabitants of peripheral regions. It is with regard to both categories that all the issues raised by the conjunction of nation, state and economy may best be illustrated, as several papers in this collection show.

This leads to a suggestion that nation-states contain their own mechanisms of destruction. The Europe of "homogeneous" nations, painfully stitched together over the last 200 years, appears to be coming apart at the seams. There are several reasons why this may be so. First, there are internal pressures. Nations were put together from many disparate local elements which had diverse reasons for accepting a national identity, if they had any reasons at all. The process of incorporation created a political and economic framework in which cleavages of the kind associated with regional movements have emerged. The activities of the state itself give rise to cleavages of a class-like kind which cut across national identity. And this is to say nothing of cleavages associated with class in the proper sense, or those which derive from the presence in the nation of migrants from diverse cultures.

There are other pressures too. The location of economic and industrial power in bodies such as multinational corporations generates activities, needs and interests which have little to do with the existing organization of national space. Supra-national institutions (EEC, NATO, COMECON), even when they are essentially congeries of more or less powerful nation-states, allow the expression of transnational interests. Few may think of themselves as "Europeans", but the reverberations at the local level may be seen, for example, in the sphere of farming. The Common Agricultural Policy makes strange bedfellows.

All the same, if organizations such as the EEC model themselves after existing nation-states, and seek "integration" — an ethnicization of polity — through the construction of common identities and cultures, they are likely to be faced with problems similar to those encountered by their predecessors. There is no reason to suppose they would be any more successful in solving them.

## Note

[1] I am grateful to Sian Reynolds, University of Sussex, who located this quotation.

## Bibliography

Ardant, G. (1975). Financial policy and economic infrastructure of modern states and nations. *In* "The Formation of National States in Western Europe", (Ed. C. Tilly), 164-242.

Ballard, R. (1978). Ethnic minorities and agencies of the state. Paper presented to SSRC "European Seminar", April 1978. Cyclostyled.

Bayley, D. H. (1975). The police and political development in Europe. *In* "The Formation of National States in Western Europe", (Ed. C. Tilly), 328-379. Princeton University Press, Princeton, MA.

Baric, L. (1968). "The meaning of citizen participation in urban renewal". *In* "Urban Renewal 1968", (Ed. S. R. Millward), Papers presented at a symposium held in the Department of Civil Engineering, University of Salford. Cyclostyled.

Bendix, R. (1977). "Nation-Building and Citizenship: Studies of our Changing Social Order", (2nd Edn), University of California Press, Berkeley, CA.

Blok, A. (1974). "The Mafia of a Sicilian Village", Basil Blackwell, Oxford.

Blok, A. (1975). "The Bokkerijders Bands 1726–1776: Preliminary Notes on Brigandage in the Southern Netherlands", Euromed, Amsterdam.

Boissevain, J. (1966). Patronage in Sicily. *Man N.S.* 1, 18-33.

Boissevain, J. (1979). Towards a Social Anthropology of the Mediterranean. *Current Anthropology* 20 (1), 81-85.

Boissevain, J. and Friedl, J. (Eds) (1975). "Beyond the Community: Social Process in Europe", Department of Educational Science of the Netherlands, The Hague.

Brandes, S. H. (1975). "Migration, Kinship and Community: Tradition and Transition in a Spanish Village", Academic Press, London and New York.

Braudel, F. (1973). "The Mediterranean and the Mediterranean World in the age of Philip II", Vol. II. Collins, London.

Causer, G. (1978). Private capital and the state in Western Europe. *In* (Eds. S. Giner and M. S. Archer), 28-54. Routledge and Kegan Paul, London.

Charbonnier, G. (1969). "Conversations with Claude Lévi-Strauss", Cape Editions, London.

Claessen, H. J. M. and Skalník, P. (Eds) (1978). "The Early State", Mouton, The Hague.

Cohen, R. (1978). State origins: a reappraisal. *In* "The Early State", (Eds H. J. M. Claessen and P. Skalník), 31-75. Mouton, The Hague.

Cohen, R. and Service, E. R. (Eds), (1978). "Origins of the State: the Anthropology of Political Evolution", Institute for the Study of Human Issues, Philadelphia.

Cole, J. W. (1977). Anthropology comes part-way home: community studies in Europe. *Rev. Anthropol.* 6, 349-378.

Craig, G., Mayo, M. and Sharman, N. (Eds), (1979). "Jobs and Community Action", Routledge and Kegan Paul, London.

Crozier, M. (1964). "The Bureaucratic Phenomenon", Tavistock Publications, London.

Cutileiro, J. (1971). "A Portuguese Rural Society", Clarendon Press and Oxford University Press, Oxford.

Daedalus, Fall (1979). The State. *Pro. Am. Acad. Arts Sci.* 108,

Davis, J. (1973). "Land and Family in a South Italian Town", Athlone Press, London.

Davis, J. (1975). Beyond the hyphen: some notes and documents on community–state relations in South Italy. *In* "Beyond the Community: Social Process in Europe", (Eds J. Boissevain and J. Friedl), 49-55. Department of Educational Science of the Netherlands, The Hague.

Davis, J. (1977). "People of the Mediterranean: an Essay in Comparative Social Anthropology", Routledge and Kegan Paul, London.

Dumont, L. (1979). "L'Allemagne répond à la France: le peuple et la nation chez Herder et Fichte. *Libre 79* 6, 233-250.

Dyson, K. (1980). "The State Tradition in Western Europe", Martin Robertson, Oxford.

Elder, N. (1979). The functions of the modern state. *In* "State and Society in Contemporary Europe", (Eds J. E. S. Hayward and R. N. Berki), 58-74. Martin Robertson, Oxford.

Finer, S. E. (1975). State- and nation-building in Europe: the role of the military. *In* "The Formation of National States in Western Europe", (Ed. C. Tilly), 84-163. Princeton University Press, Princeton.

Fishman, J. (1972). "Language and Nationalism: Two Integrative Essays", Newbury House, Rowley, Mass.

Gaulle, Charles de (1970). "Discours et Messages (3): Avec le renouveau, mai 1958–juillet 1962", Plon, Paris.

Geertz, C. (Ed.) (1963). "Old Societies and New States: the Quest for Modernity in Asia and Africa", Collier–Macmillan, London.

Geertz, C. (1975). "The Interpretation of Cultures", Hutchinson, London.

Gellner, E. and Waterbury, J. (Eds) (1977). "Patrons and Clients in Mediterranean Societies", Duckworth, London.

Giner, S. and Archer, M. S. (Eds) (1978). "Contemporary Europe: Social Structures and Cultural Patterns", Routledge and Kegan Paul, London.

Gluckman, M. (Ed.), (1964). Closed Systems and Open Minds: the Limits of Naivety in Social Anthropology", Oliver, Edinburgh.

Gordon, D. C. (1978). "The French Language and National Identity (1930–1975)", Mouton, The Hague.

Gramsci, A. (1957). "The Modern Prince and Other Writings", International Publishers, New York.

Handelman, D. (1976). Bureaucratic transactions: the development of official-client relationships in Israel. *In* "Transaction and Meaning", (Ed. B. Kapferer), 223-275. Institute for the Study of Human Issues, Philadelphia.

Hayward, J. E. S. and Berki, R. N. (Eds) (1979). "State and Society in Contemporary Europe", Martin Robertson, Oxford.

Hechter, M. (1975). "Internal Colonialism: the Celtic Fringe in British National Development, 1536-1966", Routledge and Kegan Paul, London.

Kedourie, E. (1960). "Nationalism", Hutchinson, London.

Kohn, H. (1944). "The Idea of Nationalism: a Study in its Origins and Background", Macmillan, New York.

Kohn, H. (1946). "Prophets and People: Studies in Nineteenth-Century Nationalism", Macmillan, New York.

Kohn, H. (1967). "Prelude to Nation-States: the French and German Experience, 1789-1815", D. Van Nostrand, Princeton.

Krejci, J. (1978). Ethnic problems in Europe. *In* "Contemporary Europe: Social Structures and Cultural Patterns", (Eds S. Giner and M. S. Archer); 124-171. Routledge and Kegan Paul, London.

Lafont, R. (1968). "Sur la France", Gallimard, Paris.

Lévi-Strauss, C. (1962). "La Pensée Sauvage", Plon, Paris.

Leyton, E. (1977). Studies in Irish social organization: the state of the art. *Social Studies (Dublin)*.

Loizos, P. (1975). "The Greek Gift: Politics in a Cypriot Village", Basil Blackwell, Oxford.

Macartney, C. A. (1934). "National States and National Minorities", Oxford University Press, Oxford.

Mardin, S. (1972). "Center–periphery relations: a key to Turkish politics". *Daedalus* Winter, 169-190.

Marx, E. (1976). "The Social Context of Violent Behaviour", Routledge and Kegan Paul, London.

Marx, E. (No date). Israeli society and the anthropological study of nations". (Mss.)

Marx, E. (1978). "The Balance of Power betwen Government and the Public in Israel", Paper presented to SSRC "European Seminar", April 1978. Cyclostyled.

Marx, K. (1968). The Eighteenth Brumaire of Louis Bonaparte, *In* "Karl Marx and Friederich Engels: Selected Works", 96–179. Lawrence and Wishart, London.

Mauss, M. (1969). "La nation" and "La nation et l'internationalisme". "Oeuvres 3: Cohésion Sociale et Divisions de la Sociologie", 571–639. Editions de Minuit, Paris.

Miliband, R. (1973). "The State in Capitalist Society", Quartet Books, London.

Mills, C. W. (1963). Two styles of social science research. *In* "Power, Politics and People", (Ed. I. L. Horowitz) 553–567. Oxford University Press, New York.

Pickvance, C. G. (Ed.), (1976). "Urban Sociology", Tavistock Publications, London.

Pitt-Rivers, J. (1954). "The People of the Sierra", Weidenfeld, London.

Poggi, G. (1978). The Development of the Modern State: a Sociological Introduction", Hutchinson, London.

Poulantzas, N. (1973). "Political Power and Social Classes", New Left Books and Sheed and Ward, London.

Poulantzas, N. (Ed.) (1976). "La Crise de l'Etat", Presses Universitaires Françaises, Paris.

Poulantzas, N. (1978). "State, Power, Socialism", New Left Books, London.

Rew, A. (1975). Without regard for persons: queuing for access to housing and employment in Port Moresby. *Development and Change* **6**(2), 37-49.

Rew, A. (1977). Accumulating applications: the state and shanty town property. Paper prepared for Burg Wartenstein Symposium No. 73. Wenner-Gren, New York.

Rokkan, S. (1970). "Citizens, Elections, Parties", Universitetsforlaget, Oslo.

Rokkan, S. (1975). Dimensions of state formation and nation-building. *In* "The Formation of National States in Western Europe", (Ed. C. Tilly), 562-600. Princeton University Press, Princeton, NJ.

Schneider, J. and Schneider, P. (1976). "Culture and Political Economy in Western Sicily", Academic Press, New York and London.

Seers, D., Schaffer, B., and Kiljunen, M-L. (Eds), (1979). "Underdeveloped Europe: Studies in Core–periphery Relations", Harvester Press, Hassocks, Sussex.

Seton-Watson, H. (1977). "Nations and States: an Enquiry into the Origins of Nations and the Politics of Nationalism", Methuen, London.

Shils, E. (1961). Center and periphery. *In* "The Logic of Personal Knowledge: Essays presented to Michael Polanyi on his Seventieth Birthday", 117-130. Routledge and Kegan Paul, London.

Shils, E. (1963). "On the comparative study of the new States". *In* "Old

Societies and New States: the Quest for Modernity in Africa and Asia",
(Ed. C. Geertz), 1-26. Collier–Macmillan, London.

Smith, A. D. S. (Ed.), (1976). "Nationalist Movements", Macmillan, London.

Smith, A. D. S. (1979). "Nationalism in the Twentieth Century", Martin
Robertson, London.

Snell, H. G. and Snell, T. (1975). Samish responses to processes of national
integration. *In* "Beyond the Community: Social Process in Europe",
(Eds J. Boissevain and J. Friedl), 165-184. Department of Educational
Science of the Netherlands, The Hague.

Snyder, L. L. (Ed.) (1964). "The Dynamics of Nationalism: Readings in its
Meaning and Development", D. Van Nostrand, Princeton, NJ.

Stephens, M. (1976). "Linguistic Minorities in Western Europe", Gomer
Press, Llandysal.

Strayer, J. R. (1963). The historical experience of nation-building in Europe.
*In* (Eds K. W. Deutsch and W. J. Foltz), "Nation-Building", Atherton
Press, New York.

Tarrow, S. (1977). "Between Center and Periphery: Grassroots Politicians in
Italy and France", Yale University Press, New Haven and London.

Tilly, C. (Ed.) (1975). "The Formation of National States in Western
Europe", Princeton University Press, Princeton, N.J.

Vermeulen, C. J. J. (1978). Ethnicity, nationalism and social class: The case
of the Orthodox population of Macedonia (1870–1913). Paper presented
to SSRC "European Seminar", Sept. 1978. Cyclostyled.

Wallerstein, E. (1974). "The Modern World-system: Capitalist Agriculture
and the Origins of the European World-economy in the Sixteenth
Century", Academic Press, London and New York.

Wallman, Sandra, (1978). The boundaries of "race": processes of etnicity in
England. *Man N.S.* **13(2)**, 200-217.

Weber, E. (1976). "Peasants into Frenchmen: the Modernization of Rural
France 1870-1914", Chatto and Windus, London.

Weingrod, A. (1967). Patrons, patronage and political parties. *Comp. Stud.
Soc. Hist.* **X**, 376-400.

Wheaton, M. (1979). Political parties and government decision-making. *In*
"State and Society in Contemporary Europe", (Eds J. E. S. Hayward and
R. N. Berki), 42-57. Martin Robertson, Oxford.

Yoon, S. Y. S. (1975). Provençal wine cooperatives. *In* "Beyond the
Community: Social Process in Europe", (Eds J. Boissevain and J. Friedl),
75-90. Department of Educational Science of the Netherlands, The Hague.

# 2

# *A Sense of Place*

*JEFF PRATT*

This article is a modified version of a paper given at a conference devoted to the theme of boundaries, and concentrates on the question of territorial boundaries and their importance in Italy, especially Central Italy where my own fieldwork as conducted. Even limiting the terms of inquiry in this way, it is only possible to sketch in some of the aspects of an anthropological analysis in the space available. A consideration of the importance of local loyalties in contemporary Italian life involves necessarily a historical perspective, and the first half of this paper will be concerned with historical themes. This in itself makes it necessary to concentrate on Central Italy.

The use made here of historical material is in a sense double-edged, and I shall try very briefly to make this as explicit as possible. On the one hand it seems obvious that an account of the contemporary importance of territorial boundaries and local identities has to be understood in the light of previous developments, and of periods when these factors were indeed more important than they are today. In other words it is an argument in terms of historical continuities, more crudely, in terms of survivals. But as against this, the article is also concerned to stress the qualitative difference in importance attached to local identity in earlier periods (let us say pre-Risorgimento, prior to the creation of the Italian State, though this is not the significant date for all the aspects dealt with below), as compared to the present day, and provide a contrast which will help our understanding of the contemporary pattern.

The article, then, is concerned with how territorial identities and organizational divisions below the level of the nation-state continue to play a prominent role in Italian life. It does so by illustrating in the first part the changing economic and political importance of these units in a historical perspective, and in the second part by a discussion of contemporary ideology which expresses ideas of commonality (*campanilismo*) or common interests (Christian Democrat ideology).

## Territorial Organization

In Central Italy the City-State emerged in the twelfth and thirteenth centuries, the age of the communes. Each communes consisted of a *città*, inhabited by *cittadini* (citizens) which controlled an area of countryside, and the *contado* inhabited by *contadini* (peasants). During this period the *mezzadria* or share-cropping system developed, a system which dominated the agriculture of Central Italy down to the 1950s. Land held by the Church and the rising urban merchant classes was share-cropped by the peasants who were required to be resident on the land, and whose production was directed by the landlord using customary legal contracts whose characteristics varied to some extent from commune to commune. Normally these contracts stipulated the production of certain foodstuffs for the landlord, and hence ultimately for the urban population, and to a variable extent certain other commodities for trade and industry, especially textiles.

The demographic pattern that emerged can still be seen clearly in many parts of Tuscany: a walled urban centre, surrounded by its subordinate *contado*, surrounded by the uncleared land, scrub and forest, before the next *contado* was reached. The distinction between town and country is given solid expression in the walls, whose gates were constantly manned by tax-collectors by day and shut by night. Although the walls separated *contadini* from *cittadini*, and continue to do so, their purpose was to defend the whole commune from attack. In the event of war, the peasants came to town with their livestock and the commune as a totality defended itself against other communes.

The principle can be observed in many paintings of the late middle-ages and the Renaissance. These walls, as a collective representation of the unity of a territorially defined people, recur frequently in twentieth century political ideology, and that is the reason for mentioning them here.

The communes themselves were in constant rivalry for trade, trade-routes, access to the sea and for the best agricultural land. The rivalry between them is reflected in the Guelph–Ghibbelline factions beloved of historians, a factionalism which also created divisions within the towns themselves. To be on the wrong side at the wrong time could lead to exile, as for Dante, but note that so strong is the identification with the town of birth and citizenship, that those who, for example, were exiled from Siena to Florence are still known as the *fuor'usciti di Siena* (those who have gone out from Siena) after a number of generations. (Here, as at many points, the parallel with Southern Spain is striking — see the principle of *ius soli*, mentioned by Pitt-Rivers, 1964:30.) At the simplest level we can say that a person's economic and legal rights depended very much on membership of a given town (as well as on class membership within that town), and that conversely the interests of individual citizens were subordinated to the collectivity, whether it be restrictions on commerce, usury, agricultural production or house construction. The definition of the interests of the collectivity and the composition of the ruling group varied of course with the different kinds of government which emerged during the commune period.

Some features of the rivalry between communes ended with the gradual domination and unification of Tuscany completed by the Medici in the sixteenth century. The last town to hold out against the Florentine army was Montalcino, to which the nobles of the Republic of Siena had fled. A stone in the castle records the last glorious hours of liberty before the dark days of the Florentine barbarians descended. The inscription was composed and erected in 1959.

The unification of Tuscany was a very uneven affair. If the new economic policies favoured Florentine industry, each commune, within limits set by membership of the Grand Duchy, continued to have its own tariff barriers and its own statutes and a whole mass of local particularisms. We find, for example, in the eighteenth century statutes of one small commune (Monticello, Grosseto province) that the penalty for murder or damage to property varied according to whether the victim was a native of the place or a foreigner. In the scale of fines for blasphemy, we find that the punishment varied according to whether the blasphemer was a member of the commune or a visiting stranger — in the latter case he might be banned from setting foot in the village again. (The statute is held in the archive at the town-hall in Arcidosso, Grosseto province. It is dated 1766, but is basically a copy of a statute of 1551, and very similar to a number of other commune statutes in the area.)

It would be an interesting task, though one beyond the scope of this paper, to chart historically the decline and in some cases suppression of local particularisms accompanying the rise of liberal economic policies in the late eighteenth and nineteenth centuries. In some cases the connection between economic, political and legal institutions is clear cut and the motivation apparent. For example the Tuscan Leopoldine reformers were very concerned that in the Maremma, once rich grain land, production had declined drastically through depopulation. As part of their attack on this inner frontier, the central government ordered the local communes of the Maremma not to raise taxes from settlers from other parts of Tuscany (and even from Corsica), and gave these immigrants immunity from local laws which treated more leniently crimes committed against "foreigners", i.e. decreed that the settlers should have equal rights before the law. (Renato Mori (1951) discusses at some length the innumerable taxes levied on goods transported between Tuscan communes, and how in their task of stimulating production and trade the reformers also had to tackle local particularisms in administration, law and politics. For the liberal reformers the unification of the Tuscan nation involved not just the abolition of barriers and restrictive practices viewed as feudal in origin, but a positive side in the creation of individual liberty and equality.)

In other cases the effects of liberal economic policy on local autonomy and local identities is more difficult to trace and the connections are less obvious. Some of the leading economic reformers were closely associated with the Jansenist revival in Tuscany of the second half of the eighteenth century, a revival which itself has a political dimension in terms of the desire of the Grand Duke for greater independence from Rome. Later, in the Tuscan popular insurrections of 1799, known as the "Viva Maria" riots, this theme re-emerges. The list of complaints of the rioters presents, to modern eyes, a curious mixture of economic and religious demands: jumbled together we find a demand for the restoration of tariff barriers between communes (for the "free trade" policy of the reformers had a notable effect on bread and grain prices) alongside demands for the re-veiling of religious images and the restoration of other religious institutions which had been abolished as part of the general Jansenist attack on forms of mediation between the human and the Divine. We can understand this mixture of demands as partly a result of a simple condemnation of all the policies with which an unpopular government is associated. Pietro Leopoldo supported both the Jansenists and the liberal reformers. (For material on the "Viva Maria" riots see Gabriele Turi, 1969.) But it is also possible that for reformer and reactionary alike there is a connection between the existence or abolition of economic boundaries, and the acceptance or devaluation of mediating figures — parish priest, patron saint (or miraculous image) — in a religious hierarchy. To deal with this in any detail would require an examination of the importance of the territorial organization of the Catholic Church, too large a topic to be included in the scope of this article. (For the relationship between territorial organization and the mediating figures of the Catholic Church in another context, see W. A. Christian, Jr (1972).)

If within Tuscany economic boundaries had already been under attack in the name of free trade through the liberal reformers of the Leopoldine period, the process was accelerated by Italian Unification and the growth of road and rail communication, a virtual obsession in the second half of the nineteenth century (see Sereni, 1968: chapter 1). It was accompanied by other kinds of unification, those of political and jural rights of each individual as members of that new "natural" unit, the nation-state. But if the general movement was towards political unification and the creation of a national market, various degrees of local autonomy survived, and even at the economic level some barriers remained. For example D. H. Lawrence travelling in the Maremma records the closing of the gates of Volterra every night to prevent the illicit movement of goods, and the same was true of other sizeable towns in the 1930s. The total abolition of the *dazio*, the tax paid on goods moved across communal boundaries, did not occur until 1972.

However, it is at the administrative rather than the economic level that territorial boundaries below the level of the central state machine (region, province and commune) have retained an importance greater than that found, for example, in the British system. To some extent local autonomies have been strengthened in recent years, especially by the regional reform which abolished the office of Prefect, central government's agent at the local level. This reform, promised by the post-war constitution, was approved by all political parties except by those of the extreme right (who viewed it as an attack on national identity) only in 1970. (Sicily and the northern frontiers are exceptions to this as they received regional autonomy at an earlier date.) Theoretically a great deal of power over economic planning, development agencies, health and welfare has been devolved to the regions, but as is often the case it is more the responsibility than the necessary finance which has been devolved. Even the province, the least stressed unit in the territorial hierarchy, has a certain administrative importance. For example a whole range of state employees, from teachers to post-office workers, on successfully completing an examination (*concorso*) are then entitled to a job only within a given province — whether they then receive a job in the town or village of their choice depends on luck and a complicated grading system. Geographical mobility is severely inhibited by this system. Whether a person seeks a job nearer home within the province, or wishes to move from say Milan to Turin, the outcome depends on an extremely long, cumbersome and unpredictable bureaucratic procedure.

However, it is the commune that looms largest in the lives of Italian citizens. "*Andare in comune*" (going to the town-hall) becomes a way of life, indeed for some who earn money by queuing for busy clients, it becomes a career. It is not just that a whole range of procedures from obtaining a building permit to receiving a subsidy for school transport, seem to require a personal visit to the town-hall. It is that even after the abolition of local taxes, each citizen is legally required to be resident in a particular commune, and in that commune a file is kept on a person's family status, education and occupation. This file, the *scheda de famiglia*, forms the basis of a person's identity card, is used in compiling the voting register, and also by the police. Copies of this record, obtained each time by queuing in the appropriate office (*l'anagrafe*) in the town-hall, have to accompany a host of bureaucratic requests, including, for example, any application for a state job.

One of the clearest examples of the way the Italian State attempts to "tie down" its citizens to a particular place of residence came in the aftermath of the kidnapping the political leader Aldo Moro. One of the emergency measures rushed through to combat terrorism was an obligation on all Italian citizens who absented themselves for more than three days from their commune of residence, whether on holiday or business, to register themselves in the commune where they were temporarily staying. The measures were not, to my knowledge, taken very seriously, and if they had been would have generated an amount of paperwork which was as enormous as it was useless. What is surprising is not the failure of such a measure, but the attempt, the geographical stability and local identity this and other administrative procedures assume on the part of present-day Italian citizens.

In summary, it remains true that a person's rights to pensions, medical aid, school transport and many other things can vary crucially from one local administration to another, from one side of a street to another. This section has tried to show, very briefly, how the various territorial levels below that of the nation are built into the state administration. In this sense there is some historical continuity with earlier political and administrative organizations. However, if we turn to the more purely economic aspects, we need to emphasize the discontinuities, the essential differences between the consequences of being a Florentine now and being a Florentine in the fifteenth century, whatever some of the reformers' rhetoric about renewing ancient loyalties.

## Ideological Aspects

After having discussed, in the first section, some of the issues involved in local autonomy, the second section will deal with contemporary conceptions of it, and its ideological expression.

A large number of published anthropological works on Italy make some mention of *campanilismo* (cf. Silverman, 1975; Cohen, 1977; Moss and Cappanari, 1962; Maraspini, 1968). The word implies that the bell-tower, the *campanile*, is the highest referent, the highest thing looked to, and is usually translated into English as parochialism, reflecting the pejorative overtone now present in the Italian. Occasionally we find concerned letters to local newspapers about what is admissable as local pride and what to be rejected as parochialism, but if we ignore for a moment the negative connotations of the word, the range of attitudes and conceptions associated with it are many and complex.

At the simplest level we find a conviction about the special qualities of the place and the people. The anthropologist, as stranger, meets this very early on. The people, named collectively after the place, have the best air, the finest climate, the strongest wine, or the most beautiful women, the most honest or hospitable people, or speak the best Italian, even "We are more cultured because the village was founded by the Romans", and the anthropologist should thank Heaven he chose that place rather than the one across the valley. For of course these attitudes emerge when people are distinguishing themselves from others, and are part of the rivalry between localities. Very often in Tuscany towns or villages are paired in rivalry, with scurrilous nicknames, proverbs and songs reflecting the grounds on which each holds itself superior. They often emerge into the open at village festas and dances, where visiting young men provoke fights with their hosts through abuse of their women. In many cases, such villages were endogamous, and whatever may be the economic rationality of this in terms of the inheritance of land, it is generally discussed in terms of the impossibility of successful marriages across local boundaries. In the past public disapproval of such mixed unions was institutionalized, and one or two cases indicate that the parties to such marriages were degraded as being like animals, bestialized. Even today, it is common to find that those who marry in are simply known by a nickname indicating their place of origin.

Now although these characterizations are found in a variety of settings, when we move to larger centres we find local pride combined with ideas of *civiltà*, of the superiority of town life to country life. Silverman (1975) has discussed the connotations of this word in great detail, and here I shall only mention one aspect of it. (Silverman's material on *civiltà* and *campanilismo* from Umbria corresponds very closely to my own from Tuscany, though our evaluations differ in some respects, cf. J. C. Pratt, 1973.) In Montepulciano, a small town in the province of Siena, there was a great emphasis on the town's self-sufficiency and the idea that it was a centre. This place of 4000 inhabitants contained a hospital, a law court and jail, police headquarters, tax and local administrative offices, the whole range of schools, a theatre, a bishop, and artisans producing every conceivable type of commodity, at least for the local elite. The presence of these institutions was defended against ecclesiastical and administrative attempts to rationalize local organization, as being essential to the importance of the place, and as allowing a person to live a complete life, and a civilized life, within the town walls. In this, the town is contrasted with the inconvenience of the country, whose inhabitants are outside society. *Contadini* scattered in the country are less convinced — "Those stuck up on the hill" is a generic formula for landlords, tax-collectors and other parasites.

If belief in the distinctive character of a place and its setting are very widely diffused through the population, political appeals to the unity of interests of all those defined by territorial boundaries are not. Elections in Italy are classified as either political (for national assemblies) or administrative, the election of commune councils, though in practice the political divisions and alignments are very similar in both contexts. Very commonly the Christian Democrat Party, sometimes in coalition with other right-wing groups, chooses as its campaigning symbol the commune emblem, or the walls, or the bell-tower, a symbol of the unity of the local group. It is difficult to present an account of this kind of political competition without going into specific details, but typically a list of centre--right candidates will contain local businessmen, representatives of specifically local institutions (such as the *Banca Populare* or the tourist association), a group usually having the backing of the Church, plus some claim to access to central government resources, and a claim to be the best men to look after the interests of the town and the commune. Campaigning issues are regularly those which are presented as in the interests of all those in the town or village in an undifferentiated way — improve the water supply, support the local hospital, encourage more tourism based on the natural beauty of the place and the innate hospitality of the inhabitants. The presentation of any issue in terms of sectional interests (except those territorially defined, e.g. a *frazione*, an outlying village in the commune) is avoided, as is the problem of how higher levels of administration might allocate resources — such as schools, hospitals and motorways — between competing communes.

It was mentioned above that these local elections are termed administrative rather than political, and this theme is picked up in the propaganda. Their left-wing opponents with a class ideology have introduced harmful political divisions into local affairs. The logic of this is clear — politics takes place outside the boundary. This representation is in fact very common amongst supporters of the civic lists. To take that familiar theme of the anthropological study of communities — why did the town band pack up? *"Ah, qui c'entra la politica"* (this is where politics comes in) is the reply. Some members of the band, being Communists, did not want to play in the *festa* for the patron saint of the town. The harmony of the band was disrupted by politics, conceived of as a disharmonious activity, destructive of local unities.

On some occasions we also find that the internal organization of the local unity is spelt out. The extent to which this aspect of local ideology is articulated and elaborated depends a good deal on sociological factors, but in Montepulciano, we find through the parish newspaper and election propaganda, two images of local society. Both take note of the various groupings which make up the town, but deal with them not by a class analysis, but by models of organic solidarity. One is the ancient view of society as a body-politic, where the hands (*manovali, braccianti*) do manual work and the head (*capo*) does the organizing and governing. The second also stresses the division of labour and the interdependence of the parts, and is that of the family, where the father (*capoccia* — body metaphors are present here too) directs operations, the mother does the spending, the children work hard and so on. Again we find a metaphor based on a model which like the body, is a natural unit in Catholic thought, one within which conflicts of interest are deemed impossible. But here in the model of the family we also find an explicit paternalism and a short step to the politics of patronage. To say any more about this would require an examination of the conceptualization of family relations, employer/employee relations and spiritual relations. We would need to look at Catholic social thought in general, and of course the class ideology to which it has reacted at the theological level and in specific local settings.

Organic analogies are not of course unique to *campanilismo* — in fact the body-politic image was spelt out in most detail by the secretary of the local Christian Democrat party to describe relations within his factory, and involved him in all sorts of difficulties, both of logic and of industrial relations. It is also worth stressing that although organic analogies are implicit in much of the conceptualization of social relations, we seem to find them articulated in an ideology only in particular conditions, in places of a particular size and class structure. Furthermore, although the hierarchical organic analogies are ancient, and were indeed common in the mediaeval city-states, their significance changes considerably in a modern industrial society. It is now a defensive and explicitly backward-looking ideology, as in these cases at least the bounds of the body have been broken by class action.

The final comments in this discussion of territorial unities in Italy are directed towards two other topics which go rather beyond the parish pump.

The first follows up the remarks about appeals to local loyalty and the common interests of the people of a given locality in the ideology of the Christian Democrat party. In a series of D.C. election posters from the immediate post-war period which were republished a few years ago (L. Romano and P. Scabello, 1975 — a more detailed analysis will be published elsewhere) we find this theme given pictorial treatment and used at a number of metaphorical levels. The material is rich and complex, but the main thrust of the argument is the representation of Communists as evil in a specific Christian sense, as allied to the devil, and opposed to all the traditional Christian virtues and institutions, especially the family. To this end we find the traditional walled city, familiar to us from the landscape, familiar to us from art, and as the carrier of *civiltà*, also becomes in these election posters the City of God, or at least of the Godly. In fact, of course, even this is not new, and accounts of the city-state as the City of God are to be found in Renaissance history and art. The propaganda material for the election campaign invokes citizens to defend the commune by showing a town suitably labelled with Christian virtues secure behind its walls against outsiders, the various clawed monsters and aliens who are the Communists. This enduring representation of the contrast between civilized and barbarian, good and evil, as insiders and outsiders in territorial terms, is also transposed to the national level. The walled town can also become a national symbol in this ideology, with posters representing patriotic Italians in a besieged town shutting the gates against the red hordes whose foreign connections are made suitably explicit.

The second point is concerned to qualify the implication that in political life there is a rigid dichotomy between those who think and act in terms of local loyalties, and those who have a class ideology. One of the curious facts about the Italian Communist Party (which counts a third of the electorate) is the way in which it has slowly and almost surreptitiously changed its organizational basis in the post-war period. Although party documents still proclaim that the party is organized on a cell principle, that is, essentially in the work place, on the whole this is not the case, and has not been for some time. Instead the organization is based increasingly on the sections, that is territorial units to which all those Communists resident in a given area — village or city quarter — belong, and this is so even where large-scale industry is found. On the rare occasions when this fact is mentioned publicly, it is usually explained in terms of avoiding conflicts with the trade-union organization which the Communists dominate, but within which they cooperate with other political groups. The move towards sections is also perhaps a part of the long-term strategy of alliance with other social classes which has now been blessed with the name of the *compromesso storico*. Whatever its origins, the consequence of this shift has been to create an organization which duplicates the organization and divisions of other institutions in Italian society. The result has been a curious mimicry, whereby, for example, the old pattern of village and town *festa* for patron saints has been largely replaced by Communist-run *festa del Unità*, organized by people in an area with the same boundaries as parishes and communes, with outsiders invited. The same phenomenon can be found in other areas of party ritual. I would add that this is an unstressed element in the Communist Party, but that sometimes it has had the consequence of adding an unwanted legitimacy to traditional divisions, such that these rivalries can re-emerge within the party. Thus unlucky party activists can have to deal with irate section members demanding that it is their turn to provide the commune mayor, or that not enough of the total commune budget has been spent in their village. This usually leads to a long lecture about how local loyalties should not enter into the allocation of these posts and resources. In this, party organizers are having to combat a very strong tradition, whereby, for example, it is considered entirely legitimate for Christian Democrat politicians to defend their parliamentary record and apply for re-election largely on the basis of what they have obtained for their constituents from central Government.

## Conclusion

This article has attempted to sketch some of the dimensions of territorial organizations and its conceptualization in Central Italy, using material from economic history, presentday administrative practice, political propaganda and folklore. There are many omissions, of which the most obvious is any reference to the role of the Catholic Church, as well as a lack of reference to other parts of Italy — a brief account of the 1971 riots in Reggio Calabria or L'Aquila might have dispelled any impressions that the issues discussed are limited to the villages of Central Italy, or to the more or less distant past. The article has suggested three points for further analysis:

(a) That the economic incorporation of local communities, first into the Tuscan Grand Duchy and then into the Italian nation, through the creation of road and rail networks and the reduction of internal trade-barriers by liberal reformers, was accompanied by an attack on local particularisms in the field of law, politics and religion.

(b) This process, long, slow and often opposed by the peasantry (cf. Turi on the Viva Maria riots in Turi 1969, Hobsbawm on the Lazzeretti Movement of 1878 in Hobsbawm 1959), was only partially completed. At the economic level the survival of some internal tarriff barriers was mentioned, and the virtual absence of large sectors of Central Italy's share-cropping population from the market up until the last war could be added. But it is at the level of state-administration that the survival of local autonomy, or rather the compartmentalization of the state machine, is most conspicuous, and the workings of the bureaucracy seemingly at odds with the needs of a modern industrial country. In some cases very ancient territorial boundaries have provided the units for new institutions aimed at decentralizing government — some very new wine has been poured into very old bottles.

(c) The commonality and shared interests of the inhabitants of a given locality is given ideological expression at a number of levels, and even inflects the workings of the Communist Party, though it is there devalued. At the most diffuse level, the idea of the common characteristics of a local population is expressed in the language of *campanilismo*. The idea of the common interests of a local group finds its most elaborate expression in the ideology of the Christian Democrat Party, which indeed at times behaves like an uneasy coalition of regional elites. The assumption of common interests of a local group is sometimes elaborated in organic analogies (the body-politic, the family), hierarchical models which carry the message that the distinction between governors and governed is fixed and natural. Finally the ideology of nationalism shares many of the characteristics of *campanilismo*, and in its structure and imagery is often a simple transposition of the ideology of local sub-national identities.

# References

Christian, W. A. (1972). "Person and God in a Spanish Valley", Seminar Press, New York.

Cohen, E. (1977). Nicknames, Social Boundaries and Community in an Italian Village, *Int. J. Contem. Sociol.* **14**, 102-113.

Hobsbawm, E. (1959). "Primitive Rebels", Manchester University Press, Manchester.

Maraspini, A. L. (1968). "The Study of an Italian Village", Mouton, Paris.

Mori, R. (1951). "Le Riforme Leopoldine nel Pensiero degli Economisti Toscani del '700", Sansoni Editore, Florence.

Moss, L. W. and Cappannari, S. C. (1962). Estate and Class in a South Italian Hill Village. *Am. Anthropol.* **64**, 287-300.

Pitt-Rivers, J. A. (1964). "The People of the Sierra", Chicago University Press, Chicago.

Pratt, J. C. (1973). "Friends, Brothers and Comrades", Unpublished D.Phil. Thesis, University of Sussex.

Pratt, J. C. (1980). "Christian Democrat Ideology in the Cold-War Period", Article forthcoming.

Romano, L. and Scabello, P. (1975). "C'era Una Volta La D.C." Savelli, Rome.

Sereni, E. (1968). "Il Capitalismo nelle Campagne", Einaudi, Turin.

Silverman, S. (1975). "Three Bells of Civilization, The Life of an Italian Hill Town", Columbia University Press, New York.

Statuti della Comunità de Monticello, held in archives of town hall, Arcidosso, Grosseto.

Turi, G. (1969). "Viva Maria. La Reazione alle Riforme Leopoldine", Leo S. Olschki Editore, Florence.

# 3

# *Basques, Anti-Basques and the Moral Community*

## MARIANNE HEIBERG

Social boundaries provide the interfaces for the necessary process of social classification and ordering. They are the means by which those who are perceived as "similar" are separated from those who are perceived as significantly "different". Without such boundaries social life would have little, if any, coherent shape. A system of social boundaries is as complex, fluid and, at points, contradictory as the social structure of which it forms part.

Those boundaries which are emphasized or, occasionally, newly erected — be they boundaries of class, ethnicity, religion, kinship and so forth — are responses to specific social circumstances (Mitchell, 1965; Barth, 1969). They reflect and affect the distribution of political, economic and social resources in a particular society at a particular historical moment. As such, the generation and maintenance of social boundaries implies the competition for and/or the reproduction of power (Barth, 1969; Cohen, 1969, 1974). Therefore, as the wider economic and political environment changes, the social grid of boundaries shifts accordingly although not necessarily in a direct relation. As importantly, the categories enclosed within the boundaries may radically alter in meaning and value.

This paper will deal with Basque identity and its changing function and meaning in the formation of social boundaries in the Spanish Basque country. The social boundary defined by cultural differentiation is an active, explicit feature of all realms of social life in the Basque region and most political and economic behaviour is viewed in terms of it. (However, the nature of this boundary and the cultures which it marks and separates have altered radically over the last 100 years or so. This alteration can only be understood in reference to equally radical changes that have occurred in Basque economic and political life.)

The mountainous and verdant Basque region lies in the north-west corner of Spain and is one of the most industrialized, advanced parts of the country. Its inhabitants enjoy a standard of living some 60% above the Spanish average (figure from "Renta Nacional de Espana", Banco de Bilbao). Of the approximately 2.5 million people who live in the region only around one half are Basque by descent. The remaining half came to the region as immigrants from the more impoverished rural areas of Spain attracted by Basque expanding industrial prosperity. Many of these Spanish immigrants have now lived in the Basque country for three to five generations. The vast majority of those who are Basque by descent are totally fluent in Spanish and less than 50% have a working knowledge of the Basque language, Euskera. Partly because of Euskera's legendary difficulty — it is unrelated to any Indo-European language — few of the immigrants have learnt the language.

There is a rather elaborate stereotype as to what constitutes the typical Basque. The ideal Basque should be of medium height, broad-shouldered with a triangular head and long, narrow nose. He (or she) should be born in the Basque country, have four Basque surnames (showing purity of descent for at least two generations), have his family roots in the countryside rather than the cities and, most importantly, speak Euskera. However, only a very few Basques fit into this image. Particularly in the urban centers where the large majority of Basques live, in terms of education, religion, general physical appearance and life style most Basques are — broadly speaking — indistinguishable from other Spanish citizens. Nevertheless, the inhabitants of the Basque country have been severely polarized into two ethnically differentiated, socially separated and mutually exclusive categories of people. Following the terminology of the Basques themselves, I have labelled these categories "Basque" and "anti-Basque".

This cleavage between "Basque" and "anti-Basque" must be

distinguished from another boundary which divides Basques from immigrants or non-Basques. Although a deep social division does exist between the Basque and immigrant populations — in the more rural communities the two groups tend to lead completely separate social lives — this is not the *operationally* important cleavage. One of the Basques' most revered martyrs, Juan Paredes Manot, who cried, *"Gora Euskadi askatuta!"* (Long live free Euskadi) as he was executed by Franco's police, was an immigrant who spoke no Euskera. Equally, Basque descent is not in itself sufficient to be considered by others as truly "Basque". To achieve and maintain "Basque" status requires continual and strict obedience to a certain type of social behaviour and political ideology.

## Boundary and Basque Culture: Pre-industrial Basque Society

The value placed on Basque identity — which is now a highly esteemed and sought-after commodity — and its role in dividing the social universe of the Basque country, has undergone a radical change. This change is intimately linked to a fundamental transformation of Basque society as a whole. Historically the most significant social boundary which regulated an individual's general public identity divided urbanites, *kaletara* (people from the *kalea*, or street) from the rural population, *baserritara* (people from the *baserri*, or farm). This division has far-reaching roots.

The Basque country has enjoyed three major economic assets that have profoundly patterned its entire economic and social history. These are (1) its abundant and readily available reserves of iron and lumber, the bases for the Basque iron and steel industry as well as ship-building, (2) natural, protected harbours in the Bay of Biscay and, (3) an advantageous geographical setting. The Basque country was a cross-roads between two important economic areas — England and Flanders to the north and the Castillian meseta rich in wool and grain to the south (Monreal, 1977:358). In the main, these resources were economically capitalized by the urban centers, called *villas*, which were dedicated to commerce, administrative and military activities and which linked wool and grain exporting Castilla to her external markets.

Against the advantages enjoyed by the *villas* the Basque rural hinterland has been burdened with a steep, arduous terrain and infertile soil in addition to chronic overpopulation. The poverty and high demographical density of the rural areas, together with the Basque inheritance system which transmits the *baserri* (farmstead) intact to only one heir, has induced a constant flow of people into the towns.

Economically, politically and culturally town and country in the Basque region have represented two discrete and frequently opposed social orders. The interpenetration between these two orders was minimal (Caro Baroja, 1974). Economically the compact, walled towns dedicated to administration and international commerce were set in stark relief to the dispersed and isolated farmsteads founded on domestic self-sufficiency. Politically the *villas* and the rural areas were circumscribed into different legal frameworks called *fueros*. In the main the *villas* had been established by the kings of Castilla (and later Spain) for political and military purposes and were directly tied into the Spanish monarchy. However, the rural areas were governed by elected assemblies, the *Juntas Generales*, and were only marginally integrated into the wider Spanish political apparatus.

Culturally the opposition between the two orders was as striking. Partly because of their successful participation in an international economy, the Basque mercantile classes viewed themselves as modern, cosmopolitan and illustrious. From the sixteenth century onward the Basque urban bourgeoisie were quick to adopt intellectual and technological innovations radiating out from other European countries. Vigorous, industrious, reform-minded and thoroughly Hispanized, the Basque bourgeoisie were the main agents for the introduction and diffusion of the ideas of the Enlightenment into Spain. In contrast the austere life of the *euskaldun* (Basque-speaking) rural areas was confined largely to the closed world of the rural neighbourhood, the *auzo*. The means for long-distance communication — roads, rivers, literacy, etc. — were in general lacking and contact between *auzoak* (-ak = plural) was restricted.

This duality of the Basque-speaking countryside against the Hispanized towns (although Euskera was often used as a domestic language, Spanish was the preferred public language) was frequently marked by armed confrontation. From the fifteenth century onward the Basque country was the scene of numerous peasant uprisings against urban political and economic encroachment. This process of political opposition reached its pinnacle in the nineteenth century. Throughout the major part of this century, the centralizing tendencies of the various Madrid governments combined with the aspirations of the Basque urban bourgeoisie to attack frontally the traditional

Basque political order based on the *fueros*. The foral institutions
(i.e. those founded on *fueros*) protected, by and large, a rural mode of
life and the advantaged position of the rural elites within it. The
tensions between the anti-*fuero* urban centres and the pro-*fuero* rural
areas erupted twice into bitterly fought and prolonged war. These
Carlist Wars (1833–39, 1873–76) are complicated affairs, but a few
features should be noted.

The military defeat of the rural Basques in the Carlist Wars resulted
in the abolition of the *fueros*. And foral abolition was crucial for the
development of Basque industry. Under the *fueros* the Basque
country was a duty-free zone. Customs lines were drawn along the
boundary separating the Basque country from Castilla. Therefore,
incipient Basque industry was strangled since it was cut off from
Spanish markets by heavy tariff barriers while simultaneously subject
to the uninhibited influx of competing industrial goods from abroad.
Moreover, under the foral regime the cornerstone of Basque industrial
potential — the supremely rich iron mines near Bilbao — was
communal rather than private property. After 1876 and the suppression
of the Basque *fueros*, the Basque country rapidly developed into the
second most important industrial area in Spain (the first being
Catalonia).

The modern Basque country was created by the defeat of Carlism
and the victory of liberalism and it emerged deeply divided. Foral
abolition meant the political alienation of the peasantry. It also meant
the political, economic and cultural ascendancy of the expanding
urban centres.

In this context, then, how was "Basqueness" perceived in the cities
before the impact of Basque nationalism? What was the value placed
on Basque identity? Although the vast majority of the population of
the cities prior to 1876 was Basque by descent, in Bilbao — the
birthplace of Basque industry and Basque nationalism — Euskera had
become a rarity as a spoken language already by the early nineteenth
century. The language together with other aspects of Basque
traditional culture — all part of a rural mode of life — were considered largely irrelevant to the contingencies of modern Basque
society. Miguel de Unamuno, one of the major Basque contributions to
the famous Spanish literary generation of '98, reflected widely held
attitudes when he argued in 1901 that a Bilbao speaking the Basque
language was a contradiction in terms. According to Unamuno, it
could be scientifically demonstrated that Euskera was not adaptable to
modern thought. In the main, Euskera was dismissed as the language
of the stables, the language of unsophisticated rustics, in contrast to

Spanish, the language of refinement, culture, education and urban success. Whereas Spanish historical and artistic achievements were lauded and admired, Euskera — like rural life in general — was linked to the contemptuous image of the uncultured, brutish peasant — a stigma deeply felt by rural Basques.

Euskera was mainly an oral language and its vulnerability was in part due to its lack of a literary production. In the late nineteenth century when Spanish primary schools were established throughout the Basque region, the rise of literacy and the regression of Euskera became parallel processes.

Whereas the value placed on Basque identity by the Basque urbanites was by-and-large scornful, for the rural Basques, usually illiterate and monolingual, Basque identity was accepted with mixed feelings. Their perception of the opposition between the *euskaldun baserritar* (Basque-speaking peasant) and the Hispanized *kaletar* (urbanite) was strong. On one hand the *baserritar* was regarded as a more rugged, noble being. His social code which stressed the notions of honour, social harmony and egalitarianism was perceived as a model of moral rectitude. On his isolated farmstead the *baserittar* was an independent, sovereign and virtuous individual. In contrast, the *kaletar* was viewed as delicate, dependent, tamed, manipulated and corrupt.

This vision of the moral, hard-working peasant in confrontation with the immoral, effete urbanite has had a long history in the Basque country. It has frequently been used by the Basque peasantry as a language to protest the growing power of urban elites. The ideology of peasant nobility and noble equality was given its most complete expression by Manuel de Larramendi, a Jesuit priest, in his *Corografía de Guipúzcoa* written in 1754. For Larramendi, nobility was an attribute of the land and those who worked it. The *baserritar* cultivating the land and governed by traditional rural values was the original Basque in a state of grace. It was this state of grace that had been shattered by the cities and their easy, luxurious life style. From this decadent, outside world came all inequalities and improbity.

However, the life of the street, of the urban centres, held irresistable attractions. It represented an ordered, comfortable world of regular work days, cash salaries, new housing, bars, shops, leisure and cultural excellence. It was also the world of power — of state bureaucracies, political leaders, courts, lawyers and large landlords in front of which the *baserritar*, lacking the basic skills of literacy and Spanish, was insignificant and impotent. Although the *baserritar* was perceived as more spiritually majestic, the status of *kaletar* was more desirable and prestigious. This status was an important requirement for access to political and economic resources.

To escape the drudgery and poverty of the farms, young men and women came down to the towns. hid their rural awkwardness and learnt Spanish in order through urban employment or marriage to achieve full participation in fashionable city life. From the latter part of the nineteenth century up to the present the rural sector has shrunk dramatically from some 90% of the Basque total population to less than 10%. Until the full impact of Basque nationalism made itself felt, the Basque language as well as Basque traditional culture faced extinction.

One further point: although inside the Basque country, reflecting urban ascendancy, Basque culture and identity were relegated to an inferior position, in their relations with other Spanish citizens and the Madrid political centre the Basque urbanites stressed their claims to a distinct history and culture — i.e. their Basqueness. The core of the Basque argument lay in the notion of Basque collective nobility. Against an intricate background of civil war in the Basque country and the wider military and bureaucratic ambitions of the Basque elites, during the sixteenth century all Basques were extended the legal status of *hidalguía*, nobility (see Otazu, 1973; Greenwood, 1977 for discussion). Collective nobility and the mistaken belief that Basque blood was uncontaminated by either Jewish or Moorish influences combined to create a general feeling of Basque superiority. The advantages conferred by this grant of collective nobility were immense. Noble status was an essential first step for achieving military and administrative position in the Spanish state. Noble status was an important factor in the Basques' successful economic penetration of the Americas. But, as importantly, the notion of collective nobility and hence, the special status of Basques inside Spain, were the central instruments used to maintain Basque fiscal privileges — the Basque region was exempt from all Spanish taxation — when these privileges came into conflict with the designs of the Madrid government. In short, the meaning and function of Basque status varied in accordance to the socio political boundary it served to define and defend.

## Boundary and Basque Ethnicity: Industrial Basque Society

Basque nationalism has been a dominant force in the region for some 80 years now. Although the urban centres are still the loci for the mainsprings of political, economic and social power and the rural areas are faced with a deepening crisis, the concept of Basque identity has changed drastically. Previously inside the Basque country Basqueness was essentially a descriptive term referring to cultural form judged to be of little consequence. Now the ascription of Basque status corresponds to Basque cultural content only by coincidence. In general, Basqueness has become a political category. Basque nationalism, an urban product, created Basque ethnicity and defined the rules for membership, and Basque ethnicity has created a new boundary based on the symbols of an old culture.

The general nineteenth century background for the emergence of Basque nationalism in Bilbao in the 1890s can be briefly sketched as follows. First, Spanish nationalism had shown itself to be a failed nationalism. It was incapable of over-riding intense local and regional loyalties. Because of the failure of nineteenth century liberal reforms, an economically stagnant and politically corrupt centre was unable either to inspire or control Spain's more vigorous peripheries. Secondly, the Basque country had never been a "regular" part of Spain in the same sense as Extremadura or Andalucia, for example. It had enjoyed administrative autonomy considerably longer than any other Spanish region. Also, parts of the Basque country were characterized by a culture in marked relief to other Iberian cultures. This "fact" of political and cultural differentiation provided the raw material upon which Basque nationalism drew to construct its arguments. Thirdly, the last quarter of the nineteenth century in the Spanish Basque country was a period of radical social change. The old, traditional Basque country governed by *fueros* and dedicated to commercial and agricultural enterprise was superseded by a new Basque society founded on a unified Spanish constitution and heavy, rapidly expanding industry.

In Bilbao — the Basque industrial heartland — industrialization generated extremely high social costs. Its uncontrolled and intense pace placed intolerable strains upon the social fabric of Bilbao and the whole nature of social life deteriorated noticeably. The problems of urban congestion, pollution, inflation and disease became severe. Moreover, the Basque industrial take-off created two new and politically powerful social classes. One was the Basque financial oligarchy which by the turn of the twentieth century probably formed the single most important vested-interest group in Spain. The second was the large industrial proletariat composed mainly of unskilled Spanish immigrant workers who were militant and, at times, violent advocates of socialism. Caught between these two prime movers of

Basque industrialization were the economically threatened and politically encircled Basque middle and petty bourgeoisie. It was from this latter grouping that Basque nationalism arose and would recruit its following.

Basque nationalism was inspired by a condemnation of capitalistic industrialization and led to an exaltation of traditional rural society. Although bedecked in the emotive symbols of rural society, it was an ideology constructed by urbanites to deal with urban problems. Unlike most nationalist movements, the principal attack of the early Basque nationalists was not focused on the political centre, Madrid. Its main concern was with social relationships inside the modernizing Basque country. In general, Basque nationalism has been confined to the industrial and industrializing parts of the region. Its arguments were basically aimed at two targets — first and foremost, the Spanish immigrant proletariat and secondly, the Basque financial elite. The main task of Basque nationalism — a task now successfully completed — was to transfer political and economic power away from these two social classes to those entrapped urban classes which had been peripheral to the main thrust of industrialization.

The Basque ideology is based on two fundamental assumptions:

1. The Basques and, therefore, the Basque country, constitute a sovereign nation.
2. By natural right, this Basque nation must be governed solely by Basques for the sole benefit of Basques.

However, the creation and maintenance of boundaries which would define and delimit "Basque" as a discrete and exclusive category was not a straightforward matter. A clear-cut opposition between Basques as "nationals" and Spaniards as "non-nationals" could not serve. One of the chief targets of Basque nationalism — the financial oligarchy — was Basque by descent and many of the early nationalists, as William Douglass (1971:180) has pointed out, had themselves only "shaky geneological claims" to Basque status. Moreover, for Basque nationalism to have its desired effects "Basque" had to become a politically operative category and not a static matter of once-and-for-all biological inclusion or exclusion. The opposition between Basque speakers and Spanish speakers was even less useful. Few of the nationalists spoke Euskera.

The problem was resolved through the construction of an elaborate and largely symbolic nationalist ideology. The overt historical and cultural arguments upon which this ideology rested were less important than the covert political functions these arguments were meant to perform.

The ideology can be broken down into two inter-related sets of symbols. (Cohen's definition of symbols as, "objects, acts, relationships or linguistic formations that stand *ambiguously* for a multiplicity of meanings, evoke emotions and impel men to action", (1974:23) is relevant here.) One set defined the elements of Basque cohesion and exclusiveness and consisted of Euskera, religion, traditional Basque customs and Basque character. These four elements represented the Basque mode of being in diametrical opposition to the Spanish one. Derived from Basque preindustrial society, these elements as symbols functioned to differentiate one sector of urban society defined as "Basque" opposed to other sectors rejected as "anti-Basque". Despite the nationalists' claims to the contrary, Basque customs, Euskera and so forth were not ultimately things valued in and of themselves. These symbols demarcated the battle-lines and provided "national" legitimacy in the struggle for economic and political precedence inside the Basque country.

The nationalists' view of Euskera is illustrative of the symbolic nature of the Basque ideology.

The nationalists expended considerable efforts in studying and attempting to preserve the Basque language. Among other reasons, Euskera was seen as a vehicle for the virtues of the Basque people.

"Euskera cannot be considered merely as a beautiful language worth being cultivated in literature: it is the support of our race and the buttress of the religiosity and morality of our people." — (Sabino de Arana, Epílogo, "Collected Works", p. 432)

Nonetheless, the language was not itself important.

"What is the national language, considered by itself except a simple sign by which members of a nation communicate their ideas and emotions? If it is repressed and replaced by another, the nation will continue exactly as before." — (Sabino de Arana, Efectos de la invasión, "Collected Works" p. 1327)

For the early nationalists the principal value of Euskera lay in its ability to differentiate Basques, in particular *bizcainos* (Basques from the province of Vizcaya of which Bilbao is the capital) from Latins, in particular *maketos* (the nationalists' derogatory term for Spanish immigrants). Symbolically Euskera placed a barrier of linguistic distance between Basques and their enemies.

"If we had to chose between a Vizcaya populated by *maketos* who spoke only Euskera and a Vizcaya populated by *bizcainos* who spoke only Spanish, without doubt we would select the latter (..). *Bizcainos* are as obliged to speak their national language as they are not to teach it to the *maketos* or Spaniards. Speaking one language or another is not important. Rather the difference between languages is the means of preserving us from the contagion of Spaniards and avoiding the mixing of the two races. If our invaders learnt Euskera, we would have to abandon it (..) and dedicate ourselves to speaking Russian, Norwegian or some other language unknown to them." — (Sabino de Arana, Errores Catalanistas, "Collected Works" p. 404)

The main role of Euskera — like the nationalists' conception of Basque customs, religion and so forth — was as part of the defensive armament to be used against "foreign infiltrators". In addition the nationalists also viewed these elements as underlining the opposition of the moral Basque and the immoral Spaniard. Whereas, Basque religion was a true reflection of sacred beliefs, Spanish religiosity was a mask for superstition and fanaticism. Euskera was the oldest and purist language in Europe. Spanish was *erdera*, a half-language and "bastardized degeneration". In short, the nationalists' conception of Euskera, religion, Basque customs and character provided symbols of exclusion, distance and moral differentiation which yielded ethnically and ethically separated groupings inside the Basque country. The boundary created was both a political and a moral one. In nationalist ideology the Spanish immigrant proletariat — like all things Spanish or Hispanized — was not only excluded from Basque and, hence, "national" status; it was also ejected from the moral universe.

The second set of symbols consisted of the elements of Basque history, *fueros* and the notion of Basque "original sovereignity". These elements served to separate the Basque country as a whole from the process of state unification and centralization. They provided legitimacy in the struggle over the allocation of political and economic resources between the Basque country and Madrid. Whereas, the first set of symbols demonstrated that the Basques were both culturally and morally distinct from Spaniards, the second set demonstrated that the Basque country could never either historically nor politically be regarded as part of Spain.

Standing over both these two sets of symbols and linking them together was a supreme symbol — the Basque race. The Basque race was a totally exclusive category. Race was a God-given condition that could never be achieved. Assimilation was impossible. Moreover, historic races, like the Basque, had a natural right to self-government. They were the *sine qua non* of nations.

Although race was an intrinsic attribute, nevertheless it was an attribute that could easily be lost. In nationalist ideology it was not sufficient to be Basque in terms of surnames, language or character. Ultimately it was not cultural markers that determined nationality. It was the attribute of *abertzalismo*, patriotism. The over-riding feature of the nationalist stress on race was a concern about political loyalties. Political loyalty meant unquestioned public fidelity to the political goal of Basque differentiation, exclusiveness and preference. The Basque ethnic community was viewed as a moral community. The moral duty of all "Basques" was the economic and political defence of this community. In other words, a *real* Basque — a Basque with full national rights — could only be a Basque nationalist.

Clearly the Basque financial oligarchy whose economic behaviour had brought with it the massive inflow of Spanish immigrants and whose political behaviour depended on strong links with Madrid were placed firmly and irrevocably into the camp of the "anti-Basques". For the Basque nationalists the Basque industrialists were responsible for, "all the immorality, blasphemy, crime, free-thought, socialism anarchism (...) that is corrupting the Vizcayan soul".

Whereas, in the rest of Spain political life has broadly operated in terms of the left versus the right, Basque politics has been determined by the complex interactions of three discrete political options — the non-nationalist right, the nationalists and the non-nationalist left.

By the outbreak of the Spanish Civil War in 1936 the Basque nationalists commanded one-third of the electoral vote. The remaining two-thirds was evenly divided between the nationalists' two traditional opponents — the socialists, supported by the immigrant workers and sectors of the Basque working class and the right-wing parties, supported by the Basque economic elite. Both these latter two political forces each from their own vantage point viewed the nationalists with undisguised hostility. The socialists were appalled at the nationalists' arch-conservatism, ethnic exclusiveness and frantic religiosity. The Basque right-wing parties ridiculed the nationalist claim to a monopoly over Basque status and, therefore, Basque "national" resources. If the nationalists were Basques, by all geneological evidence so were the Basque financial oligarchy.

The repression the nationalists in particular and the Basques in general suffered under the Franco regime was brutal. Thousands were imprisoned or forced into exile. Many were executed. Moreover, Franco viewed Basque culture largely as an excuse for and sign of separatism. Therefore, the regime unleashed a thorough campaign of cultural repression. The public use of Basque greetings, traditional garments, folklore, names, publications and the teaching of Euskera were strictly forbidden. These measures were enforced by a vast array of new pro-Franco officials who exercised a stringent control over all aspects of public life. Under the force of the Franco regime Basque nationalism was paralysed into dormancy.

## Abertzales *and* Españolistas: *the Renovation of the Basque Moral Community*

When Basque nationalism slowly resurfaced in the 1960s, its ideology in certain aspects had shifted dramatically. Previously the nationalists had declared Socialism and Socialists to be anti-Basque and anti-Christ. However, the young nationalists who emerged with ETA (*Euzkadi'Ta Askatasuna*) proclaimed themselves Socialists as well as nationalists. This conversion was in part inspired by the model of Third World anti-colonial struggles and the European student movements. On the non-nationalist side of the political divide attitudes had also changed. Due to the increasing visibility of minority nationalisms in Europe and the deeply hated centralism of the Franco period, the idea that the Basques formed a distinct nationality and had an inherent right to some sort of sovereignity — i.e. to be governed by Basques only — became profoundly acknowledged by the non-nationalists. As a reflection of this attitude most residents of the Basque region claimed Basque status. Such a claim was regarded a moral obligation and a political necessity. Thus, at Franco's death in 1975 the nationalists and the left-wing non-nationalists appeared to be united in a broad agreement concerning the desired relationship with Madrid and in a common front against the various Basque right-wing parties.

However, Basque nationalism was and is not just a struggle for territory, for Basque autonomy. More importantly, Basque nationalism supports arguments for a *differential* relationship between certain sectors of the population and others inside the Basque country. It is a struggle for power within a territory occupied by two different political orientations. When competitive politics again became possible in Spain, this struggle for precedence — for exclusive political ownership over economic and social resources — erupted in full force. But Basque nationalism implies a very special form of competition. It is strictly non-oecumenical. In nationalist doctrine, the "national" — or nationalist — community should have control over the resources of the "national" territory by natural right.

The symbols of Basque nationalism had been transformed to accord

with new European intellectual doctrines. The concept of Basque
culture replaced the Basque race as the central symbol of Basque
identity and exclusiveness. Basque Socialism substituted Basque
Catholicism as the defining element of Basque morality and innate
social justice. (see Sarrailh de Ihartza, 1973 for fullest exposition of this
view.) But the covert political functions behind these new symbols
remained unchanged. The nationalist conception of Basque culture,
language, Socialism and so forth, continued to be subordinate to an
exclusive political loyalty summed up in the term *abertzalismo*
(patriotism). For the Basque nationalists only an *abertsale* (patriot)
could be a true "Basque" and only a Basque nationalist could be
an *abertzale*.

Despite the apparent agreement in political platforms — both
nationalists and non-nationalists demanded Basque autonomy,
amnesty for Basque political prisoners, sweeping social reform, official
bilingualism and measures to revive Basque culture — the social logic
of nationalism bitterly polarized Basque society into *abertzales* and
*españolistas*. All aspects of public life — newspapers, schools, popular
festivals, academic research, publishing houses, artistic production,
amnesty organizations, labour unions as well as political parties were
categorized into *abertzale* — *españolista*, Basque–anti-Basque,
national–non-national.

A fuller consideration of Basque politics, which are exceedingly
complex, falls outside the confines of this paper. However, one aspect
should be noted. The "Basque" side of this cleavage is replete with
internal conflicts and tension. Politically it ranges from the Christian
democratic Basque Nationalist Party, by far the most important party
in the Basque country, to the Marxist–Leninist ETA. Despite political
fragmentation and disparities, however, the nationalists perceive
themselves as forming a political family bonded by a shared moral
cause. On the level of political action the unity forged by nationalism is
much stronger than the disunity generated by political conflict.

In contrast the "anti-Basque" side of this boundary does not have a
separate, coherent existence. It is a category created by nationalism
into which a wide range of disparate groupings are placed. These
groupings — which include the Spanish police, the Communist and
Socialist parties of Euskadi, Basque industrialists and so forth — have
no shared interests, ideology, identity or political ambitions. On no
level do they combine for the purpose of political action. Moreover,
with the exception of the Spanish police, these groupings fiercely reject
their "anti-Basque" label.

The boundary created by this division between *abertzales* and *españolistas*, or anti-Basques, is currently successfully being used to establish the lines of a differential access to public resources. A Basque home-rule statute was granted in 1979 and at present all key public positions in both the political and economic spheres are occupied by nationalists. Many Basque non-nationalists are beginning to fear that this structural inequality of access to public resources may eventually generate tensions in the Spanish Basque country similar to those experienced in Northern Ireland, with equally tragic consequences.

## Acknowledgements

This paper is based on research originally funded by the Social Science Research Council. I should like to thank Ms Gill Shephard for her valuable comments.

## References

Arana-Goiri, S. de. "Obras Completas", Sabindiaf-Batza, Buenos Aires.

Barth, F. (1969). "Ethnic Groups and Boundaries", Universtetsforlaget, Oslo.

Cohen, A. (1969). "Custom and Politics in Urban Africa", Routledge and Kegan Paul, London.

Cohen, A. (1974). "Two-dimensional Man", Routledge and Kegan Paul, London.

Caro Baroja, J. (1974). "Introducción a la Historia Social y Económica del Pueblo Vasco", Txertoa, San Sebastian.

Douglass, W. (1971). "Basque Nationalism", Pi-Sunyer (Ed.), *The Limits of Integration: Ethnicity and Nationalism in Modern Europe.* Research Reports nr. 9, Dept. of Anthropology, University of Massachusetts.

Greenwood, D. (1977). Continuity in change: Spanish Basque ethnicity as a historical process. (Ed. D. Esman), "Ethnic Conflict in the Western World", Cornell University Press, Ithaca, New York.

Larramendi, M. de (1754). *Corografía de Guipúzcoa.*

Mitchell, J. C. (1956). "The Kalela dance", Manchester University Press for the Rhodes-Livingstone Institute, Manchester.

Monreal, G. (1977). Las instituciones vascas. "Cultura Vasca I". Erein, San Sebastian.

Otazu y Llana, A. (1973). "El 'Igualtarirismo' Vasco: Mito y Realidad", Txertoa, San Sebastian.

Sarrailh de Ihartza, F. (pseud.) (1973). "Vasconia", Norbait, Buenos Aires.

## 4

# *Educational Aspirations of Ethnic Minorities: Slovenes in Italy*

*L. F. BARIC*

## *Introduction*

Aspirations for higher educational qualifications are frequently to be found in ethnic minorities. The relationship between educational attainment and occupational status is complex, but it is still widely accepted that higher levels of education lead to higher prestige jobs. Despite the prevalence of educated unemployment in parts of many countries (for example India, see Blaug, 1970), education is still felt to be a route to wealth and higher status.

It is therefore puzzling when further education in a minority language is largely rejected, as was the case in the Trieste Province of Northern Italy in the late 1960s, where the Slovene-speaking minority did not fully take advantage of the possibilities for advanced education. The situation could readily be understood if such education were available only in the majority language, and not in that of the ethnic minority. But this was not so in Trieste, where provision was made for education in Slovene, including the Slovene Scientific

College, the Slovene Teacher Training Institute and the Slovene Technical Commercial Institute.

It cannot therefore have been the case that the local Slovene population feared the erosion of their language tradition through being forced to accept higher education in Italian. The question was much discussed by planners and educationalists in Trieste Province at the end of the 1960s, and became the starting point for the research on which this paper is based.

The study is a contribution to historical ethnography: much has now changed in the area, and the 1960s situation must be seen against a background of violent political feeling about the location of the frontier between Italy and Yugoslavia. The disputed frontier was a legacy of the Second World War. The problems of the province were perceived by the Italian authorities of the time as being largely economic, since they were determined not to return the area to Yugoslavia. It was widely felt that all would be well, provided the depressed economic level could be raised.

The apparent lack of dynamism of the Slovene population was therefore a serious problem in the light of Italian policy for the area. Education was seen as a valuable basis for development, and the improvement of knowledge and skills interpreted as a prerequisite for growth. Explanations of the situation were many and varied, but popular ones took the form of arguing that the Slovenes did not have the right psychological attitude, or that they were locked in a culture of poverty. In the course of the research, it became clear that the answer lay less in individual psychology than in the nature and processes of the maintenance of boundaries in relation to national identity.

The approach required the bringing together of a number of available methods of research, which combined a participant observation study carried out in one village, a random sample of villages (excluding border villages and the intensive study village from the sampling frame); a questionnaire survey of a random sample of 240 households within the village sample; interviews with local officials, political leaders, priests, school teachers, academics and prominent citizens in the Slovene area and in Trieste; content analysis of the region's mass media; and library research using local materials. I was much assisted by two research assistants and an excellent survey team. Trieste Province consists of the large town of Trieste and the smaller town of Muggia, with coastal villages containing largely Italian populations and upland villages in the karst (limestone) hinterland with largely

Slovene populations. In a relatively small area, all the problems of national conflict, frontiers, the maintenance of ethnic cultures and the problems of promoting economic development exhibited themselves. The work reported here reflects only one aspect of the overall set of problems eventually studied.

## Education and Minority Groups

### Identity

The rejection of education in a foreign, majority language is understandable. Education through the medium of a particular language transmits the conceptualizations and values of the culture of which the language is part. This reproduction of cultural characteristics may occur without any conscious intention on the part of the educators, or it may be combined with true indoctrination. The resistance to conversion to another culture is then a straightforward means of preserving ethnic identity.

In order to move beyond this simple notion and explore rejection of education in the ethnic language, it is necessary to consider more closely its relationship to identity. The notion of identity involves the idea of contrast, as has been pointed out by Epstein (1978), who discusses the dual or "we" and "they" aspects of ethnic identity. It is immediately worth asking whether the Slovene population in Italy rejected education as being incompatible with their historic identity as peasants.

For evidence on this, it is possible to turn to the survey of 240 village households taken from a random sample of villages in the karst region. The villages surveyed were Sgonico, Sales, Prosecco, Rupingrande, Contovello, Aurisina, Trebiciano and San Dorligo.

One of the aspects explored in depth in the household survey was the value of education. A total of 40% of respondents thought that their educational level had been too low. It was the case that education was largely seen in terms of the acquisition of skills linked with the practical problem of work, but there was no suggestion from any of the data, field and observational as well as survey, that the Slovenes thought in terms of being simple peasants and workers, rather than "educated people". It was quite consistent with the image of their identity to accept the value of education. It is not therefore reasonable to assume that there is a "not for us" explanation of the general lack of enthusiasm. It was interesting and unexpected to find that about half the sample population (heavily biased towards male heads of households) thought there should be no difference between the level and type of aspiration for education for boys and girls. I would accept this figure with some caution since the survey and research team consisted largely of females and this may have affected results. But it does underline the point that education was in general acceptable and compatible with the Slovene ethnic identity, and not in itself problematical.

It is necessary, then, to look to other strategic areas for an explanation of the "education problem".

## The advantages of education

While the Slovene group may have seen no inconsistency in being a highly educated minority, it may have been the case that there were strong practical reasons why education beyond elementary school was not seen as being worth pursuing.

It was clear, however, that the Slovenes saw education as being an important key to status and wealth. They had high aspirations for their children and were willing to help them in their school work in any way possible. (It is important to realize that parents are expected to take a much larger part in the education of their children in Continental Europe than in England.)

The pattern of change in occupations among the Slovene minority follows a path that is familiar, from a phase in which the major occupations were peasant landholder or unskilled labourer (usually agricultural) to a phase in which the major form of occupation was as a skilled or unskilled employee in industry, through to a phase, already beginning in the late 1960s but now greatly extended, in which service industry and white-collar occupations have become more important. Nevertheless the former peasant cultivation as a type of livelihood still provided about half the households with a greater or lesser contribution to the household finances.

The role of education in this change was seen as very important. A large proportion of members of the population thought it was related to type of occupation, income and the ease of finding work. Children had to be encouraged in their education. Only 15% of respondents thought that children should not be helped by parents with school work and pressed to attain higher levels. The rest accepted a responsibility as parents to push children, and to convince them of the need for qualifications and knowledge.

There was considerable optimism about the economic future of the area (which, at that time of the research, seemed subjective rather than reflected in the actual situation), and the optimists also tended to be in favour of the need for more and better education.

The overall conclusion from the combined evidence of survey and field work was that there was a good deal of abstract enthusiasm for education after elementary school. The total of 67% thought there should be more provision available at this higher level (even though demand for existing provision might not be sufficiently utilized).

It is quite possible for people to combine a theoretical keenness for education with an actual choice that reveals a gap between the image and the practice. Such apparent inconsistencies did not concern the Slovene minority any more than analogous inconsistencies concern other groups elsewhere. But this discussion leaves us still looking for an explanation of the decisions taken in practice, on the parts of children and parents. In order to explore this, we need to turn to the actual events and situations of the time, to ask what was the experience of people with higher levels of education.

## Education and opportunity

The perceived opportunities to make use of higher education depend on the socially constructed reality of the people concerned. As Stinchcombe (1978) has argued in his interpretation of "virtual choices" (roughly equivalent as an idea to Popper's "situational analysis" (1972)) that an important aspect of this reality is provided by the "concrete historical materials" (p. 62). It is thus necessary to look at both what appears to have been the situation, and how it seemed from the perspective of the Slovenes in the area.

This requires a sketch of the main socioeconomic characteristics of the area affecting the Slovene group. I have referred to the Slovenes as a minority, and so they are, in the area as a whole; but within the upland region they form a majoriy. Their area is distinctive in its Sloveneness. At the end of the 1960s, villagers made up communities in the strong sense: working, living and playing all in the same limited region. The local pubs were centres of contact and activity, where only Slovene was spoken, and Italian outsiders, if they appeared at all, were extremely noticeable.

Networks of friendship and kinship were dense and well maintained. Religion served to intensify ties, since Slovenes in Yugoslavia are traditionally Roman Catholic, and there was thus no conflict in this aspect of their being settled in Italy. Family rituals, such as christenings, weddings and funerals were important, as was Christmas and Easter. Nevertheless, the radical and progressive views of many of the population were reflected in the low ranking of the profession of priest, and in a certain anticlericalism in the district.

The local community was both supportive and a valuable resource, since employment and assistance followed kin and friendship lines, in the manner familiar to all those who have studied Mediterranean societies.

Strong language loyalty was a very important feature. A total of 93% of respondents spoke Slovene in households. Some members of households spoke both Italian (usually Triestino dialect) and Slovene at home. This was sometimes the case where husband or wife was Italian in origin. The use of Slovene was a sign of familiarity and domesticity. Within the family, Slovene itself was differentiated according to the appropriate variation for talking among and to children, and among and to adults of different sexes. This variation is most easily encompassed in the most familiar language. As Fishman (1972) has pointed out, referring to Fischer (1958), in most societies children talk differently to parents and to friends. Furthermore "one of the frequent comments about American travellers abroad is that they know (*at most*) only one variety of the language of the country they are visiting. As a result, they speak in the same way to a child, professor, the boot-black and a shop-keeper, thus revealing not only their foreign-ness, but also their ignorance of the appropriate ways of signalling local role relationships". It is possible to operate in a social sense more flexibly and freely in a language in which a number of variants are controlled.

Within the local community, national language use is the most important diacritical sign of group membership. When naming their group, members of the local population often used the phrase "we Slovenes" or "we in Italy", but the phrase "we Italians" was not used. The preference for Slovene did not imply that the Slavs could not speak or understand Italian, either "high" or Triestino. Some Slavs spoke Italian at work. Some 42% of respondents in the survey thought that schooling in two languages had helped them in the work they obtained. But as many as 86% of respondents thought that as far as the present young generation was concerned, Slovene would help rather than hinder the young in their future lives and occupations.

On the administrative level, the separation of Italian and Slovene in the province falls into the category usually called diglossia (see Ferguson, 1959). The official recognition of two or more languages as legitimate varieties for communication can lead to a linguistically stable situation, in which the languages coexist, without great change or conflict, for long periods. This is well documented, for example, in the case of Switzerland (see Steinberg, 1976). In Devin (Duino), where the intensive field study was carried out, official notices were posted in both Slovene and Italian. But this was not a completely balanced diglossia, in that Italian was noticeably dominant in official, local government business. Since such matters tended to be localized in the towns (Trieste/Muggia), which were largely Italian speaking, it appeared natural to the town residents for this to be the case.

The preservation of the identity of linguistically based groups is less problematical where diglossia prevails, because of the stability provided by official sanction. But many diglossic situations appear fraught with conflict; this is because social movements and pressure groups are engaged in promoting the recognition of one or other of the languages. Where there is this precarious diglossia, language is most likely to become a focus of nationalistic feeling. It was certainly the case that the Slovenes felt that all notices, official business and so on, should be in both languages, although they recognized that this would be unlikely to make much difference to the use of Italian in occupations and commerce.

On the level of the individual speaker, bilingualism provides at least two methods of interacting, one in either language. (It is also possible, as mentioned above, to have a variety of modes within one particular language). It is also possible to have diglossia without bilingualism, and vice versa, but the comparative data most relevant to frontiers are derived from situations where both diglossia and bilingualism prevail. An impressive feature of bilingualism is the uniformity with which the ranking of communications settings is preserved, when situations in different societies are compared. A good deal of the research on the subject fits the paradigm worked out by Rubin (1968) (who has revealed a number of branching categories of usage: location, rural, non-rural, formality, intimacy, seriousness of discourse, first language learnt, language proficiency, sex). Some similar type of classification (adding class or status) can be devised to fit most field studies. The regularity of usage of Slovene as compared with Italian was clear within the group. These different usages in different contexts could serve as markers in the process of boundary maintenance. A sudden shift in language could indicate a change in the perceived situation. Accompanying a "cultural leader" informant to see an official, a Slovene who was referred to as his close friend, I found the language in which we were conversing shifted from Slovene in the ante room, waiting to see the official, to Italian in his office, to Slovene in the office when the official's assistant left, to Italian when the official was bidding us farewell in the corridor. It is possible to see quite clearly that language in use is not a passive reflection of boundaries preserved between groups on the basis of other forms of social action, but is a steering mechanism in its own right.

This maintenance of boundaries between the category of Slovene residents and others is not a one-way process. It is true that the question of identity is much less important to the Italians *vis-à-vis* the Slovenes. Many Italians in the province are unaware of the size and cultural distinctiveness of the Slovene population. Many Italians I spoke to in the course of the work were surprised at the number of villages which were almost wholly Slovene speaking. The situation nevertheless needed to be treated as a consequence of action and response on the part of both Slav and Italian speakers. For the most part, Italian speakers at the end of the 1960s saw the Slav population as an undifferentiated group, relatively unskilled and backward, from which they exempted those members of the group known to them personally, especially the "cultural leaders". Most niceties of Slovene linguistic usages, together with the role relationships involved, escaped them completely.

It was not in fact the case that the Slovene community was homogeneous. In Devin (Duino), the very great differences in cultural orientation of the rich Slovene businessmen, radical intelligentsia, unskilled workers and innkeepers living on the tourist industry, emerged clearly. This makes me doubt whether it is adequate to treat any ethnic group as homogeneous. This is how Barth (1969), in his concentration on boundaries, treats the "cultural staff" that the boundary encloses. The maintenance of cultural boundaries is more important to some categories of the population than others. In the case of the Slovenes, the "cultural leaders" had a great influence on the general views of the population. They were not, for a variety of reasons, strongly insistent on encouraging the population to aim for higher education.

We have, therefore, a picture of a differentiated but cohesive group strongly maintaining its boundaries — a resource offering both material and non-material support. An individual rejecting this group had quite a lot to lose.

It is necessary to turn now to the political and economic situation in the area.

Politically "hot" frontiers are interesting from an economic point of view. The insecurity of border regions may lead to denudation and decline. On the other hand, it is frequently in the interests of each nation state to develop each side of the frontier and secure it with settlements of satisfied citizens. The existence of a frontier in itself provides opportunities for work, such as administrative services, trading activities and tourism. Trieste is at present one of the main shopping centres for North West Yugoslavia, and was so even in the 1960s.

The problem in the Trieste region was one of lack of industry. Although the city is a great port, and has an international scientific institution and a university, the hinterland is largely empty. In order to make use of qualifications the more educated Slovenes had to leave. Many tried to get work in Trieste itself, but this was difficult and unemployment levels were high. The greatest possibility lay in obtaining work in the industrial cities of Northern Italy, such as Milan or Turin.

The Slovene population appeared to misjudge the situation, to some extent, in that they expressed highly optimistic views about the region's economy. Nevertheless the experience they reported when it came down to actual cases could have been enough to convey a message. Asked about their knowledge of the fate of anyone with higher education, 54% of respondents said that the people they knew had had to move away from the region in order to get work, and 7% knew others who had had to migrate abroad. Many with qualifications did not get adequate work. Only 16% knew of people who had found better possibilities of work within the area after they had obtained higher qualifications.

Those who left the community and the area were thought to lose touch and disappear into the Italian population, sometimes, it was reported, changing names after one generation.

It was a hard practical question, then, whether the loss of the ethnic community support, which could not be maintained at a distance, since it was based on simple daily contact and services in one part of the country, could be balanced by the chances of improved wealth and status supposedly arising from attempts to gain educational qualifications.

Of course, the people involved did not see the situation in these terms and coolly weigh up advantages. They thought in terms of leaving family and friends and going away to face a chancy future elsewhere. The inconsistencies and ambivalent views about education, aspirations and economic opportunity are all compatible with the reality of their situation.

## Conclusion

If we look now at the aggregated consequences of the acceptance of higher education, we can see the effect is not to enhance the status of the group, but, as generations succeed each other, to tend to destroy it as an entity. A few members of the group who thought about the problem as a whole, especially the "cultural leaders", were well aware of the process. One such leader told me that in the past he had thought it desirable to encourage people to try to "better themselves" but now he no longer did. This conscious policy is also connected in complex ways with the nationalist aspirations of Slovene political leaders. It is difficult to know to what extent the leaders' views may have influenced individual decisions among ordinary families.

The conclusion must be that, given the economic situation in Trieste Province, the price of gaining and using higher educational qualifications was likely to be withdrawal from the local community. Rejection of the proffered educational opportunities was not an explicit choice made in order to preserve the community as an entity, but, in aggregate, that was its effect.

## Acknowledgement

This research was supported by a grant from the Social Science Research Council.

## References

Barth, F. (ed.), (1969). "Ethnic Groups and Boundaries: The Social Organization of Culture Difference", Universitets Forlaget and Allan and Unwin, London.

Blaug, M. (1970). "The Unemployment of the Educated in India" extracted from "An Introduction to the Economics of Education", Allen Lane, London, 1970, reprinted in R. Jolley, E. de Kadt, H. Singer & F. Wilson, "Third World Employment, Problems and Strategy", Penguin Books, Harmondsworth.

Epstein, A. L. (1978). "Ethos and Identity: Three Studies in Ethnicity", Tavistock and Aldine, London/Chicago.

Ferguson, C. A. (1959). Diglossia, *Word* **XV**, 325-340.

Fischer, J. L. (1958). Social Influences in the Choice of a Linguistic Variant, *Word* **XIV**, 47-56.

Fishman, J. A. (1972). "The Sociology of Language: An Interdisciplinary Social Science Approach to Language in Society", Newbury House, Rowley, MA.

Popper, K. R. (1972). "Objective Knowledge: An Evolutionary Approach", Clarendon Press, Oxford.

Rubin, J. (1968). Language and education in Paraguay. *In* "Language Problems in Developing Nations", (Eds J. A. Fishman, C. A. Ferguson and J. Das Gupta), Wiley, New York.

Steinberg, J. (1976). "Why Switzerland?" Cambridge University Press, Cambridge.

Stinchcombe, A. L. (1978). "Theoretical Methods in Social History", Academic Press, London and New York.

# 5

# *Social Workers and Immigrants in Lyon, France*

R. D. GRILLO

This paper is based on fieldwork carried out in the city of Lyon in 1975–76 for a SSRC-financed project originally concerned with class, status and ethnicity among immigrant workers (see Grillo, 1978). Such research in anthropology has often focussed on what are construed as immigrant "communities" and provides a perspective, as it were, from the inside looking out. Such a perspective, invaluable though it is, was found in Lyon to be less fruitful than one which focussed on the receiving society and its institutions, and examined their significance for a society's members of whom immigrants are but one instance. Lloyd's (1978) comments on Watson (1977) and Watson's remarks on Castles and Kosack (1973) illuminate the advantages and disadvantages of these two perspectives.

Contemporary France, in this case the receiving society, has been described by sociologists such as Touraine (1974) as "post-industrial", a term which has been widely and variously used in recent years (e.g. Bell, 1976; Kumar, 1978) to characterize our present type of "advanced" system in which production and consumption take a

73

particular form. The concept cannot be examined in detail here, but certain key features may be mentioned briefly.

There is an especial emphasis on the organization of consumption, both individual and collective, what Lojkine calls "the totality of material supports of the activities devoted to the extended reproduction of social labour power . . . medical, sports, educational and public transport facilities" (1976:121). "Consumers", a term which may be used very broadly, engage in a wide variety of relationships homologous to employer–employee relationships in production: landlord–tenant, doctor–patient, teacher–pupil, salesperson–customer, social worker–client. This may seem a highly heterogeneous collection, and the differences must not be underestimated, but:

(a) Many of these relationships are increasingly located within the framework of large-scale bureaucratically ordered "institutions" — schools, hospitals, housing authorities, property companies, supermarkets.

(b) Many of these institutions are state-controlled, or as in the case of France, state-supported and state-orientated in many complex ways even when not state-owned.

(c) Such institutions control important basic resources (housing, education, welfare), and for many people access to such resources is channelled via such institutions.

(d) Some of the institutions both control and organize the consumption of such resources, and concern themselves with the activities of persons as consumers or producers. That is, they operate on relations of production and consumption.

(e) The institutions and their personnel are frequently engaged in the application of scientific and social scientific knowledge through which they seek to understand and mould the relations on which they are operating.

It is with these last two aspects of state or state-inspired institutional activity that this paper is ultimately concerned. It thus touches on the nature of the functionary–client relationship with which some other papers in this volume also deal. The immediate aim is, however, more limited in that I concentrate on how one type of functionary, the social worker, in one type of institution, perceives one type of client, the North African immigrant. That is, it presents only one part of a very complex picture, and raises more questions than can be answered here. The paper should also be seen as a contribution to the more specialized literature on social workers and immigrants which has emerged in recent years (e.g. Ballard, 1979; Fred, 1979; Handelman, 1976).

## *Immigrants in Lyon and the Organization of the Social Services*

In Lyon there are some 200 000 first- and second-generation immigrants in a population of around 1.2 million. About half come from North and West Africa, and the rest mainly from Southern Europe. The North African population has nearly doubled in the last decade with a substantial increase in the numbers of families. This influx coincided with a programme of urban renewal guided by the late mayor, Louis Pradel (see Lojkine, 1974), which entailed considerable disruption of the central area. Between 1968 and 1975 (census years) there was a net fall of 20% in the population of this area, a figure which underestimates total movement as there has been some new residential construction. This new housing in the central area, however, consists mostly of high-cost apartments that replaced aged tenements which previously provided cheap accommodation for immigrants and others.

The restructuring of the centre has been accompanied by suburban growth, in middle-class zones to the West, and in working class areas to the East, where are located two *Zones à Urbanizer en Priorité* or "ZUPs", at Vaulx-en-Velin and at Vénissieux. The ZUPs are very large planned housing estates — that at Vénissieux has a population of 40 000. The housing stock consists mostly of *Habitations à Loyer Modéré* ("HLM") — low-rent subsidized housing erected and owned by a variety of public, semi-public and private organizations known as *Offices* or *Sociétés*. The two ZUPs, which date from the late 'sixties, have over 20% immigrants in their populations.

Like others in Lyon immigrants have been caught up in the process of urban renewal. Their position in the housing market has been particularly affected. The demolition of privately owned tenements to which they had relatively easy access means that accommodation must be sought increasingly in institutionally controlled housing: hostels for single men, and for families apartments owned by large property companies, or more usually by the HLM. The social services have an important role in this process of "institutionalization".

The term *"travailleur social"* covers a wide range of persons. There are, however, three main categories: the *assistants sociaux* (social assistants), *éducateurs*, and *animateurs*. Each has its own distinct history, organization, training, type of personnel, task, and philosophy. *Educateurs* operate in small teams attached to a particular quartier and work "dans la rue", as they say. *Animateurs* — "animation" is a

key term in French urban planning — organize group activities in a
social centre. This paper is concerned mostly with the third category,
the social assistants.

Social assistants, mainly women and mainly middle-class in origin,
are trained at one of 36 schools in France, following a three-year
diploma course usually after the "Bac". The nationally regulated
syllabus prescribes a mix of theoretical and practical units including
some medicine, law, sociology, economics, psychology, etc. After
training the assistants find jobs in a variety of public and private
organizations, including industry. In the public sector the main
employer is the *Direction Départementale de l'Action Sanitaire et
Sociale* (known as the "DDASS") which, together with the *Caisse
d'Allocations Familiales*, is the principal state institution concerned
with welfare in all its forms. The DDASS is a huge organization with
many branches, the most important from our point of view being the
*"Protection Maternelle et Enfantile"* section of *"Enfance et Maternité"*
in which most of the assistants are located. Assistants controlled by this
section are allocated to *"Circonscriptions"*, areas which roughly
coincide with a commune, in turn divided into *"Secteurs"*. In the
secteur the *"personnel de base"* is often organized in *"équipes
polyvalentes"* of medical, psychiatric and social workers working from
a social centre.

There are also two important private, publicly subsidized organizations
which specialize in immigrants: the *Service Social Familial Nord
Africain* (SSFNA), concerned historically with Algerians, and the
*Service Social d'Aide aux Emigrants* (SSAE) which deals with other
nationalities and which also specializes in administrative problems.
Social work of various kinds is also undertaken by bodies such as the
*Notre Dame des Sans Abri* (NDSA), a Catholic organization based in
Lyon which runs many of the *Cités de Transit* (temporary accom-
modation centres).

In an urban *quartier* one may find a multiplicity of social work
organizations and personnel, public and private, operating side by
side. Not infrequently this gives rise to situations of the kind reported
by the SSFNA for one *quartier* where each of the 150 North African
families with which it had contact was, on average, being "followed"
(jargon term) by three different services.

Although social workers may in a sense be marginal to the lives of
most ordinary French families, they are of central importance to
immigrants, especially those from North Africa, because of the extent
to which the services participate in certain administrative procedures.
Any immigrant family which legally enters France, or has an illegal
entry "regularized", is the subject of a series of *"enquêtes"* which seek

to establish its "suitability" for entry. Contacts thus established are maintained after admission. Social workers also participate in the housing system, especially in processing applications for HLM. They also engage in what is called "socioeducative action" among mostly immigrant families placed in *Cités de Transit*. Such action is designed to prepare the families for life in an HLM on a ZUP. Families which have recently acquired HLM accommodation are also "followed". Social workers, especially the social assistants, therefore operate at two important points of access: entry into France, and entry into public sector accommodation. In ordinary day-to-day activities too, the social assistants find themselves working extensively with immigrants dealing with "problems" of a medical, social or administrative nature.

Social assistants are in the forefront of the machinery which the French state has developed for handling immigrants and other "marginal" social categories. "We are the executive agents of the institutions", I was told, a role which sometimes conflicts with what is conceived to be that of their profession. They are also integrated at local and national levels in policy formation. Their assessment of the "problems" of immigrants, and how to deal with them, is incorporated via a series of consultative committees where they often see themselves acting as "intermediaries" between immigrants and the authorities.

The relationship between national and local policies — their elaboration and execution — is a complex one which can be discussed here only indirectly. One may begin, and I stress it is a beginning, by examining certain ideas expressed by social assistants. These ideas occur in remarks, conversations, reports and discussions focussing on the activities in which the assistants engage. The analysis is concerned less with "what actually happens" than with what social assistants think is happening, that is with their conception of immigrant society and their role towards it. The analysis is necessarily partial, not least because it omits any consideration of the conceptions of the clients.

In quantitative and qualitative terms, the most important "interventions" (jargon) that social assistants make concern North African women, and the rest of this paper is devoted to these. Understanding such interventions requires first some assessment of the image that assistants have of the North African family and the status of women within it.

## Social Assistants and North African Women

A report prepared for the NDSA divided families in *Cités de Transit* into two main categories. There are those within which there is "entente, dialogue et collaboration sur des bases de réciprocité", and

those which are: "unis, sans conflit . . . mais la femme a dans le foyer
un rôle subalterne et inférieure par rapport à l'homme qui la domine:
il s'agit presque uniquement de foyers maghrébins . . . beaucoup,
originaires du milieu paysan, restés eux-mêmes très paysans dans leur
psychologie et leur regard sur la nature et le temps . . . l'autorité de
l'homme et la soumission de la femme sont de règle . . . servante d'un
mari grand seigneur." (Lapraz 1972:86).

The cyclostyled Annual Report of the SSFNA's Lyon branch for
1974 comments on visits to the homes of North African women
"traditionnellement tenues à rester au foyer sans contact avec
l'extérieure . . . la majorité des familles Nord Africaines quittent sans
transition une mode de vie traditionelle et presque toujours rurale,
pour passer dans un monde 'étrange', qui ni leur mentalité, ni leur
éducation, ni leur entourage immédiat ne les incitent à effronter
directement. De plus la plupart ne parlent pas français, n'ont pas été
scolarisées et ont la tendance à se replier sur elles-mêmes." (p. 4).

The following remarks come from various social assistants.

> "Muslim society is a community of men who find it less difficult to live
> separated from women than we do. Women have a difficult role in Muslim
> society — sexually and in terms of their relationship with men."
>
> "In Algeria there is practically no life as a couple. There is a world of
> women, their life, their own world. Not everywhere of course. In some
> milieux that's changing. Here the woman finds herself in a nuclear family,
> and eight children on one's own are more difficult to bring up than 25
> children shared between three. And the women are called on to do more
> things. The husband here sees his authority diminished. He is devalued."
>
> "The men live separate lives, do not share their lives with their wives, go
> out without telling their wives, do not tell their wives how much they earn
> . . . In traditional Muslim society the wife doesn't exist. Her role is to bring
> up the children. Her horizons are hardly broadened. In France they don't
> know where they are, they're really lost . . . They have little *'ouverture
> d'esprit'*. They are not even conscious of their own inferiority."

Summarizing these and other such comments, we may piece
together the following representation of North African families. They
come from rural societies, "straight from the *bled*", with a traditional
way of life which is at variance with that of French society, specifically
that of French urban families. This traditional life implies, among
other things, certain attitudes towards hygiene, children (large families
brought up in a system of discipline at once too severe and not strict
enough), women (segregated and subordinate), and adherence to
customary practices which are often considered shocking ("slaughtering
sheep in the bath"). Many "problems" stem from this.

Some of the comments may seem "anthropological", and in a sense there is a kind of anthropology which underlies the representation outlined in the previous paragraph. We return to this later. Meanwhile, let us describe what we have as a "two-culture" model of North African families in France. The model consists of various statements about culture, in the anthropological sense. The implication that there are other models using other kinds of statement should not be missed.

What might lead some to distinguish this model from anthropological models of similar type is that it evaluates a contrast between two cultures and uses that evaluation to judge the possibilities for the *"adaptation"*, *"assimilation"*, *"insertion"*, or *"intégration"* of North African families in French society. These concepts are of central importance to the rhetoric, at least, of French policy. Another, which forms part of this set, and which is often found in the language of social assistants, is one which will be familiar to those with any knowledge of French colonial history. It is a term which refers to the changes thought necessary to bring about the transition from one culture to the other, changes which the social assistants themselves might effect; *"évolution"*.

> *"Evoluées* are women who can keep up with what happens in the apartment, who make out for themselves, who know what services to approach for help, who know the purpose of domestic appliances, who can look after their money, who take themselves in hand, look after their children . . . The *évoluée* is someone capable of knowing what must be done with her children, who doesn't seek to stay in her hole."
>
> "The *évoluée* refuses to accept any longer to stay in the house. She aspires to another form of life."
>
> *"Evolués* refers to people who have acquired a certain level of comprehension, of integration. Not many are *évolués*. With *évolués* you can discuss. For the most part people work, go home, watch TV. The children are dressed correctly, fed, looked after, yes. But they never think about the future, about economic and political problems. This is not unique to immigrant workers. To be not *évolué* means to have a very low intellectual level. They do not seek an *"ouverture"*. It is partly a matter of I.Q., and partly of not having had the possibility for developing the intellect, perhaps through study . . . The Moroccans are more *évoluées* (than the Algerians), one says, because the majority have been to school, know how to read and write. They have an *'ouverture d'esprit'*."
>
> "The Algerian mother goes out very little, mixes very little. The child goes to school and frequently evolves more quickly than the mother. Regarding *évoluer*, sometimes I tell myself, after all, to evolve is to adapt. Integrate? Does this mean take our manners, our European customs? Evolve, for us, like us? Is that an *évolution*?"

There are several terms which go together: *évoluer, ouverture d'esprit, ouverture culturelle, sortir* (in a physical and social sense). Another is "autonomy":

> "An evolved woman is an unveiled woman . . . Autonomy means in comparison with her traditional upbringing which crushes her. Liberation would be a better word. Autonomy also refers to the place of the family in French society, means that they have a better knowledge of French society, are better placed to use the facilities. It means independent, free to choose Muslim culture if they wish".

| *Traditional, North African* | *Modern, French* |
|---|---|
| Woman constrained | Woman free |
| Children free | Children constrained |
| Segregated, enclosed, passive, subordinate | Autonomous, open, active, equal |

EVOLUTION

*Fig. 1 Two images of woman*

At its simplest, *évolution*, a process, may refer to becoming like the French (*"Evoluées* really refers to women who have taken on our customs"), though there are numerous indices of this: independence of spirit, from the social services, egalitarian, shared, relationship with the husband, education, fluency in French, a job, bringing up children in an approved fashion, keeping track of their progress at school, maintaining a clean flat and filling it with consumer durables, and so on. It is not unusual to be told of particular individuals who are singled out and described as *"évoluée"*. Again at its simplest, *évoluée* refers to the kind of woman a North African ought to become, in the eyes of the assistants, and I would argue that, with certain exceptions, the assistants work to create such a person. These are the images with which they operate. See Fig. 1.

That the production of the evolved woman is their goal emerges not just from the statements and reflections of the social assistants, but is apparent in their actions, in their handling of their clients. It is also apparent in the courses they organize. The SSFNA holds a range of classes which are carefully modulated and adapted to women at different stages of evolution. The woman moves progressively from being helped with domestic matters on an individual basis in the home, to small group activities such as sewing and cooking (described as "basic techniques and knowledge which allow the participants to have access to a real autonomy"), to more ambitious and structured programmes of study dealing, for example, with birth control. "The pill is the symbol of *évolution*."

There is, then, a two-culture model which entails two images of woman, the transition from one to the other (*évolution*) usually seen as a progression. To explore in detail the components of these images is beyond the scope of this paper, where it is possible only to sketch an outline of the principal elements. We have also been concerned mainly to document the ideas held by social assistants, what they think rather than what they do. However, some brief consideration at least of what they believe to be the practical consequences of their work is illuminating. The following paragraph attempts to summarize the assistants' own reflections on, and assessment of, their interventions, though I am aware it may read as if it were an observer's analysis of such interventions.

The "problem" of North African women springs from what is conceived to be their position in Muslim culture as separated from and subordinate to men. The aspirations of North African women are thwarted by the men who seek to maintain their women in their traditionally subservient position. Thus any activity which seeks to encourage changes in that position has profound effects on the man, and on his roles as husband and father. Social assistants are much exercised by the "problems" of teenage girls. In brief, such girls experience a period of acute crisis at about age 16 when compulsory attendance at school ends. At that point the girl has to reconcile what might be the demands of her family, not least of her father, that she marry, with her own aspirations to continue her education, or get a job. The school, the social assistant, and the environing society tend to support her. By encouraging such girls, or by acting as a channel through which their grievances can be expressed, or simply by allowing them to be used by such girls, the social assistants intervene against the North African male as father. In the same way, by encouraging mothers to evolve, by supporting demands for contraception, say, they throw their weight behind wives against husbands.

That "interventions" may pose a moral dilemma is sometimes recognized. "Our work allows (North African women) to show their children that they can read and write. The danger is that we create needs in them, and in some cases I know the woman has revolted.

Do we have the right to do this? On the individual level, no. But if the issue is placed in historical perspective, yes . . . If one puts oneself in the historical context (of Algeria), I, as a woman, have the right."

The person who made that remark, as assistant of the SSFNA, was also the one who employed the term "liberation" in a quotation cited earlier. The use of that word, with all its ideological connotations, may begin to suggest the inadequacy of the presentation thus far. Consider the following comments derived from conversations with a number of social workers employed at a *Cité de Transit* in a South-western suburb.

> "Women should gain a certain autonomy through the courses. We refuse to be a place where people just consume. There must be possibilities for autonomy . . . The important thing is that we make people conscious of their exploitation, of the fact that there are means . . . In the literacy classes the monitrice is directing women's attention towards the female condition, so that they take control of themselves, become aware of this condition."

> "The immigrant woman has a double alienation, as woman and as immigrant . . . One starts with dress-making and so on, which is what the women demand. The immigrant women do not want to become militants of Women's Lib. They want to make clothes for their kids because they have to save money. One tries to exploit that to the maximum. From then on one tries to find how they can become mistresses of their own situation, to become conscious."

An examination of such remarks, and a closer examination of those cited earlier, would reveal many nuances in the views of social assistants for which we cannot account in detail here. In brief, intertwined with the two-culture model described earlier are other models. The most recent series of quotations reveals this clearly. For behind these utterances is at least one other model which, if it shares some of the assumptions and elements of the two culture perspective, is in other respects very different. The vocabulary — *"exploitation"*, *"aliénation"*, *"prise de conscience"* (which may be contrasted with *"ouverture d'esprit"*), even the use of the French word which has here been translated as "immigrant" (i.e. *"immigré"*) — indicates that we are listening to utterances based on a model whose elements may be construed as belonging to a left-wing (*gauchiste*) ideological corpus.

There is an obvious point here, but it needs to be stressed. There is a great variety of views held by social assistants concerning immigrants and other persons. What the earlier discussion of "evolution" has documented is just one perspective. But it is an important one in that it forms part of a dominant, or at any rate predominant, ideology. We return to this below. That within the social services individuals and groups can and do operate with different ideologies, some of which do not reflect the predominant position, is of considerable importance, not least for the clients. A full analysis of the implications of this, and of the activities of the loose cross-service groupings of social workers and others who share similar ideological leanings and a common interest in immigrants, is beyond the scope of this paper.

We must discuss further the significance of what I have termed the predominant ideological position as that is reflected in the two-culture model. To digress for a moment, however, it should first be made clear that what has been presented here is a simplified, ideal-type version of that model. It is an analytical construct which is rarely found in a pure form in "reality". Actual ideological utterances are much more complex, flexible and above all eclectic than that. An example is provided by the assistant whose remarks are cited on p. 80 ("An evolved woman is an unveiled woman . . .") and on p. 81 ("Our work allows . . ."). Professor Lorraine Baric (personal communication) has pointed out that the first quotation, in particular the last sentence, reveals an intriguing contradiction. For in what sense can an "evolved" ( = "free" woman) choose Muslim culture ("which crushes her") and remain "evolved"? In part, this derives from a contradiction in official policy, which talks now of a kind of assimilation, now of a kind of cultural pluralism. The assistant's sentiments echo this. However, as the second quotation perhaps indicates, the informant is, ideologically speaking, somewhat eclectic, and employs a variety of different models. Systematic presentation of a model obscures such variation. But then, to add another twist, such systematization, which for the anthropologist is an analytical device, does exist in the society in question. For the systematic refinement of ideology forms an integral part of French intellectual culture.

In what sense may the two-culture model be termed predominant? And what has this to do with the state and state institutions in a "post-industrial" society? First, a simple and frequently expressed view is that social work is at the service of the society which pays for it. "The authorities see the police as the stick, the *éducateurs* as the sugar". It is more complex than that, but undoubtedly the social services form part of the apparatus of social control and social guidance in the broadest sense. Although part of their task is to handle what are defined as awkward cases, there is another part which is more positive or creative in that their activities encourage their clients to adopt certain types of social role and engage in particular kinds of social relationship. Emanuel Marx in his study of the town of Galilah in Israel comments:

"Public workers . . . demand that children should be clean, properly
fed, neatly dressed and equipped for school etc." (Marx, 1976:69).
Their concern, however, as is that of the French social assistants, is
always with much more than just hygiene. For example, the Lapraz
report, cited earlier, describes two Algerian families. One of them
evokes a favourable comment:

> "Présente un logement propre, bien rangé: lits avec draps propres,
> appartement décoré, plantes vertes, fleurs artificielles, TV, mobilier de
> salle à manger . . . chambre à coucher . . . en contre-plaqué avec
> enjolivures. Le ménage est organisé, les enfants contrôlés . . . La cuisine est
> restée algérienne, mais le foyer dispose d'une voiture avec laquelle homme
> et femme vont faire ensemble les achats dans les supermarchés." (Lapraz
> 1972:130).

It can be argued in a straightforward way that the values which
social workers seek to encourage are at least consistent with those which
are dominant in the wider society. This also applies to the ideological
framework through which they conceptualize their task. The
two-culture model illustrates this in a number of ways. Consider, for
example, the implications of a model which stresses "cultural", as
opposed to other elements (e.g. economic, political), in its interpretation
of the situation of immigrants. Furthermore, if we look closely at the
nature of the persons said to be "evolved", we can see that in certain
respects they and their families represent the ideal units for a society
which organizes production and consumption in certain ways:

> "On peut dire que les foyers qu'abrite la cité sont en bonne voie de
> reclassement. Les vêtements des adultes et des enfants, la possession
> d'appareils ménagers de modèle récent, de la télévision, de voitures
> mêmes, en sont une preuve. Par ailleurs, les intérieurs sont, dans
> l'ensemble, bien tenus avec parfois même une netteté et un ameublement
> qu'envieraient bien des foyers lyonnais." (NDSA comment quoted in
> SLPM 1969:61).

Thus, putting it at its crudest, the two-culture model maps a route to
progress (*évolution*) which North African families and others must
follow if they are to become fit "consumers" (and "producers") in
French society. This is, I believe, one of the implications of what
Article 14 of the European Social Charter has defined as the role of
social action to assist migrant workers, i.e. action which "contributes to
the welfare and development of both individual and groups in the
community, and to their adjustment to the social environment." (cited
in Council of Europe 1968, p. 9). What I have described as a "left-wing

model" in part presents what its proponents would see as an alternative to this perspective.

In France the social services play an important role with regard to persons as consumers of one major resource: housing. For reasons which cannot be discussed here, the French housing system, through the *Sociétés* and *Offices HLM*, provides a certain type of urban accommodation — units of a certain size and type, architectural design, physical location, etc. — and urban environment. Over the last 15 years this has often meant a two- or three-bedroomed flat in a large apartment block on a massive housing estate. The pattern is not unfamiliar in some British cities (e.g. London, Liverpool, Glasgow). Such housing, it is thought, can only function as intended with a population of given social and demographic structure. People have to be "trained" to live on such estates, and such training is given quite consciously to North African and other immigrant families. That is what "socioeducative action" attempts to do.

So the function of social workers as "executive agents of the institutions" is, more often than not, to concern themselves with persons in their roles as producers and consumers, especially the latter. They operate on relations of public (and private) consumption. This view is consistent with that of Emanuel Marx (personal communication) who has suggested that the social services are concerned with making immigrant families accessible to their own and other institutions, for example the schools. One social assistant commented on the difference, in her view, between Moroccan and Algerian families: "The Moroccans are more '*évoluées*' than the Algerians. One has more entry into their families". This entry is essential if the institutions are to carry out their allotted tasks. To expand a point made earlier, social workers in Lyon act as "gatekeepers" at a point of access for families and individuals to the institutions and the resources they control, and vice versa.

The characterization of social work and social workers which emerges from this discussion is, it must be recognized, a crude one, and may imply a somewhat jaundiced view of social welfare activities in a society like France (or Britain), and the state's role in their organization and distribution (cf. Poulantzas 1978:189). It should be stressed once again that not all social workers share the same values, and many would see themselves as working towards quite other ends. Leaving aside those who are avowedly "leftist", there are many who would define their roles, and orientate their actions, by reference to professionally defined aims which are incompatible with what has been described here as the function of social work. This conflict of aim and function may for them be a real source of tension.

There are other conflicts too which this paper in concentrating on a rather static analysis of the aims and attitudes of social workers which they attempt to put into practice has glossed over. For example, that social workers may be described as "gatekeepers" suggests that their relations with clients should be seen as a micropolitical resource struggle in which many other parties are involved: the different fractions of the state at local and national levels, municipal government, political groups, residents' associations, housing societies, construction companies and so on. There is a much more complex relationship between ideas and their enaction than that which has been discussed here.

Let me end with two general comments on the nature of the "ideologies" of social workers. These always entail a social *policy*, i.e. a programme for social relationships, which in many cases reflects the policy of the society at large. Social policies must, almost by definition, rest on certain *sociological* assumptions, and in our societies are likely to be articulated in a quasi-sociological form. This is partly what I meant when I suggested that the social assistants' representation of North African families seemed very "anthropological". It is at the very least a kind of "folk anthropology", though it is one which is likely to be informed by the academic training in social science which social workers undergo. That, however, raises the difficult question whether the views we have examined have been shaped by formal academic anthropology, which has passed into popular tradition, or whether anthropology itself is shaped by the popular tradition, or rather by the assumptions on which that tradition rests and which anthropology shares.

This links with a final point. Daniel Bell (1976) has argued that the systematic application of scientific and technical knowledge to production is one of the characteristics of "post-industrial" societies. This is well known and documented. Less well documented is the systematic application of the "soft" sciences — psychology, sociology, anthropology. On the ZUP at Vaulx-en-Velin, among the first appointments with the architect-in-chief and the *"paysagiste"*, was that of a sociologist. Social workers trained in social science provide just one instance of what in urban France is a very widespread phenomenon. However, whereas it might just be argued that technology is harnessed to create and improve products for the consumer, the soft sciences may operate the other way round, to create the consumer for the product.

# References

Ballard, R. (1978). "Some aspects of the response of state institutions and their personnel to immigrants in Yorkshire". Cyclostyled.
Ballard, R. (1979). "Ethnic minorities and the social services: What type of service?" "Minority Families in Britain", 147-164. (Ed. V. Saifullah-Khan), Macmillan, London.
Bell, Daniel (1976) "The Coming of Post-industrial Society", Penguin Books, Harmondsworth.
Castles, S. and Kosack, G. (1973). "Immigrant Workers and Class Structure in Western Europe", Oxford University Press/Institute of Race Relations, London.
Council of Europe 1968, "Social Services for Migrant Workers", Strasbourg.
Fred, M. (1979). "How Sweden works: a case from the bureaucracy. "The Social Anthropology of Work", (Ed. S. Wallman), 159-175. ASA Monographs 19, Academic Press, London and New York.
Grillo, R. D. (1978). Report to SSRC on Project No. 3410/2.
Handelman, D. (1976). Bureaucratic transactions: the development of official-client relationships in Israel. *In* "Transaction and Meaning", (Ed. B. Kapferer), 223-275. ASA Essays in Social Anthropology 1, Institute for the Study of Human Issues, Philadelphia.
Kumar, K. (1978). "Prophecy and Progress: the Sociology of Industrial and Post-industrial Society", Penguin Books, Harmondsworth.
Lapraz, Y. (1972). "Etude sur l'évolution des familles en cités de transit". Cyclostyled.
Lloyd, P. C. (1978). Review of "Between two Cultures", (1977). (Ed. J. Watson), Basil Blackwell, Oxford, in *R. Anthropol. Inst. Newsletter*, April 1978.
Lojkine, J. (1974). "La Politique Urbaine dans la Région lyonnaise, 1945-72", Mouton, Paris.
Lojkine, J. (1976). Contributions to a Marxist theory of capitalist urbanization. *In* "Urban Sociology", (Ed. C. Pickvance), 119-146. Tavistock Publications, London.
Marx, E. (1976). "The Social Context of Violent Behaviour", Routledge and Kegan Paul, London.
Poulantzas, Nicos (1978). "State, Power Socialism", New Left Books, London.
S.L.P.M. (1969). "Groupe de Synthèse de Promotion des Migrants", Lyon: Service de Liaison et de Promotion des Migrants. Cyclostyled.
Touraine, A. (1974). "The Post-industrial Society", Wildwood House, London.
Watson, J. (Ed.) (1977). "Between Two Cultures", Basil Blackwell, Oxford.

# 6

# Regional Policies in Italy for Migrant Workers Returning Home[(1)]

*AMALIA SIGNORELLI*

During the century which has passed since the establishment of national unity in 1870, 26 million Italians have emigrated abroad — to the Americas, Australia and European countries. Not all those who have taken part in this exodus of biblical dimensions have settled abroad permanently. Even if globally the number of those emigrating has greatly exceeded that of those returning to the country, there has been a continuous and quite consistent flow of re-entries. These returning migrants have until recently been ignored by the Italian state, by the trade unions, and by researchers.

It is not just a question of retired people who return to their country rich in savings, allowances and experience: on the contrary, these make up quite a small proportion of returning emigrants. From the last century onwards more substantial trends towards re-entry can be seen among two other categories: emigrants with seasonal or temporary work contracts; emigrants who return "spontaneously" after a period of varying length spent abroad. Often they have accumulated savings on which they hope to live, rarely have they obtained abroad a professional qualification which they hope to use in their own country. Sometimes they have neither of these and return more or less in the condition in which they left (Barbagallo, 1973; Signorelli *et al.*, 1977; Doxa, 1973).

We shall begin with a brief look at the transformation in the official position of the state towards returning emigrants. I shall then describe some research on which I am presently engaged and which is as yet incomplete. I should stress that the data and the discussion concern Italian emigration to Europe after the Second World War. Italian emigration to other countries, and the immigration to Europe of other ethnic groups, may have many different characteristics.

## The Evolution of Policies Concerning Returning Emigrants

Italian governments have always encouraged emigration. It was, in fact, a useful and economical system for ensuring social peace in a country which had begun late the process of industrialization and had decided to allocate the major part of its modest resources to the development of a single productive sector and in a single geographic area.

Emigration from Italy to Europe and the other continents exploded after the political unification of the country, when for a variety of reasons which are not examined here, the living conditions of the rural population, and especially of that of the South, grew markedly worse. Emigration abroad was only halted in appearance by the fascist regime. The decision to halt emigration did not spring from any modification of the model for development adopted for Italy. However, instead of sending unemployed and landless agricultural workers over the ocean, Mussolini had the idea of dressing them as soldiers, and of sending them to conquer a piece of land to cultivate in Africa.

After the Second World War, reconstruction and the industrial boom increased the demand for a cheap work-force in all the areas where development was concentrated. Italian "peasants" began once more to leave their own villages, going first again to America and Australia, than in ever-growing numbers to the so-called industrial triangle of Italy, and the EEC countries. Once more Italian governments thought that in this exodus they had found the solution to a problem of development, and adopting the theory under which the lightening of the demographic load was a condition *sine qua non* of the socioeconomic take-off of the depressed areas, they encouraged the emigration of the masses in every way.

As for the opposition forces, the trade unions were preoccupied by the weakening of contractual power in the internal labour market brought about the existence of a mass of unemployed and under-employed workers; the marxist parties held that emigration was a vehicle for the process of proletarianization of the rural masses. So, while demanding greater concern for emigrants and less oppressive working conditions, neither parties nor unions put forward a concrete policy against emigration. As a consequence, the offical policy of the Italian state has been to accept emigration and to work for the protection and care of Italians abroad, but also to encourage their permanent settlement in the country of immigration. For those who return, there has been no policy at all.

This situation has changed since the end of the Sixties. A decisive element has been the establishment of the Regions. The regional governments, which are decentralized and much more in touch with local social realities, were obliged to face two facts. In depressed regions a few industrial undertakings promoted by state intervention had been consolidated. But emigration had left them isolated, making markedly worse the demographic, urban and ecological conditions of whole districts, without there being, in exchange, an improvement in the productive conditions and the productive structures in agriculture. The other fact which the Regions had to recognize was the consistent presence of emigrants who returned (on average 30% of expatriates, even in years when emigration was at its highest), and who brought back with them savings and experience, but also problems and difficulties, e.g. adults looking for work, and children with problems of adaptation.

The beginning of the recession in the Western economy led to a progressive growth in the return flow. In the period 1971–74 those returning were 80% of those emigrating and in 1975 as much as 144% (Malfatti, 1976). In consequence, between 1973 and 1974 the Regions issued laws favouring returning emigrants and set up Regional Advisory Councils for emigration, whose participants are local administrators, trade unionists, representatives of political parties, members of the emigrants' associations, researchers and experts. In 1975, the First National Conference on Emigration was held in Rome. This was the first, although not entirely successful, attempt to construct a coherent emigration policy. Taking the aspects which interest us, the Conference recognized the existence and the consistent nature of repatriation, and the need to formulate a policy for returning emigrants which takes into account their real situations as revealed by the most recent social and economic research. It is recognized that the existing regional laws are inadequate and at present Regions from which emigration takes place are engaged in reformulating the laws and in relating their policy for emigrants to their real needs.

The research which I am presenting was, in fact, initiated by the Puglia Region, whose government intends by so doing to gain the necessary knowledge for changing the law on the re-entry of emigrants and to plan a policy which favours them according to new criteria.

## General Hypothesis at the Basis of this Research

Some researchers have explained repatriation by reference to certain individual characteristics of the emigrants, such as age, level of education, area of origin and so on. For Alberone and Baglioni the ability of the immigrant to integrate himself into industrial society is connected with the content of his socialization: the more socialization precedes the experience of emigration and characterize it as positive, the greater are the possibilities that the immigrant will integrate Alberoni and Baglioni, 1963).

Similarly Blumer and other authors hold that what they call "the myth of returning", which persists in the culture of emigrants, constitutes a notable obstacle to settlement and integration in a foreign country (Blumer, 1970).

In my view, in examining the behaviour of emigrants (and indeed any other social phenomenon) it is necessary to analyse a double order of causes: cultural or superstructural ones, such as the cognitive map, value orientations, models; but also the economic and social, that is structural ones, such as relationships of production, productive forces, the system of roles.

In the case of emigrants we can start from an observation *a posteriori*. Many emigrants would appear to be insufficiently socialized to be integrated, but not one of them was ever so asocial that he could not be put to work, and exploited. Why then, after a time, was it that some immigrants could remain and others not?

Migration is less the result of individual initiatives, or of the excess of workers in countries from which emigration takes place, than the by-product of the development model adopted by advanced industrial countries. This statement is validated by at least two facts: any reduction in production in the country of immigration quickly transforms the entry flow into a flow of return to the country of origin; if, vice versa, the necessity of importing a greater number of workers is shown, countries forgotten until that moment are requested to activate migratory flows (Blumer, 1970; Mottura and Pugliese, 1975; Castles and Kosack, 1973).

From this structural point of view an immigrant becomes integrated or not for reasons quite other than his psychological attributes. The stability of his employment depends on the extent to which it is profitable to keep him or to dismiss him; and this in turn depends on a combination of many factors such as his own skills, and the level and nature of the productive process in which he is employed. Vice versa, an emigrant who returns is not so much a man without qualities, as a unit expelled from a sector or a productive level, occupation of which is kept precarious by the system.

Even the situation in which they find themselves when they have returned home should, I think, be defined first in structural terms. Before discussing whether they are re-inserted or maladjusted, if they are happy or unhappy to be home, we must ascertain what their condition as workers is.

Our hypothesis is that they will be either unemployed or under-employed, or in precarious employment and underpaid. We can add that probably many of them (but not all) have some savings, a small capital sum which could be invested. But this fact gives rise to another problem: what conditions for utilizing this capital can be offered by a socioeconomic area like those to which the emigrants return?

We have thus defined an initial area in which the relationship between the community of emigrants and the state institutions must be analysed. These are the relations of production which the emigrants enter as members of the work-force and/or holders of modest capital sums. The state and its local organs enter here as the institutions which formulate general decisions on economic policy, and at the local level particular decisions concerning firms, investments, the setting up of work, the concession of credit and incentives, etc.

It is evident that the analysis of relations of production can only be accurately carried out with the help of an economist. The task of the anthropologist is to analyse the cultural links between the community and the state institutions.

On this subject it is worth setting out briefly some theoretical points which are at the basis of my working hypotheses. In this research, the term "culture" is used in a restricted sense, not as a synonym for civilization or society, but rather as a synonym for *Weltanschaaung*, "mentality". Culture is a cognitive and valuative system, a mental structure by which we succeed in knowing and judging and in deciding how and why and for what to act.

By adopting this definition, we have aimed to obtain the following results:

1. to define an area of homogeneous phenomena, mental in nature even if socially determined, which can be studied by standardized instruments, thus obtaining comparable results;
2. to emphasize that, if culture does not include the totality of social reality, but is only one level of it, we need a body of theoretical hypotheses which define:
   (a) the other levels (economic structures, social structures, psychological structures, etc.), and
   (b) the reciprocal links and conditionings between the different levels.

Apologising for the brevity of this summary, I should add that under point (2) I refer to the fundamental hypotheses of Karl Marx on the modes of production of social reality, that is the relations between productive forces and relations of production considered as the basis for the definition and the characterization of collective social subjects (classes, social strata, groups, etc.). I refer also to his hypotheses concerning the conflict (latent or manifest between collective historical subjects) since they are the bearers of antagonistic interests, and to the consequent hypothesis relating to the nature of domination and submission, appropriation and alienation, hegemony and subordination which the links between social subjects take on. Finally, I refer to the group of hypotheses concerning the relationship between conflict, conservation, reproduction and change — that is, history (Marx, 1970, 1971; Marx and Engels, 1972).

According to the hypotheses of Marx, culture should be defined as social consciousness, which means, as Marx himself would say, "social reality taken as a system of ideas", or, precisely, as *Weltanschaaung*, a mental system through which we become conscious of the social reality of which we are part. This obviously means that there will be a link between the collective historical subjects which make up a social system and the stratification and articulation of culture; and that culture will have a role both in the relationships of domination and in the processes of change.

I accept, however, as a working hypothesis, the autonomy of culture with regard to social and economic structure. Culture is not simply the "mirror" of social structure. It does not, simply, "reflect" the structure. Culture has its own particular action on social reality through the processes of legitimization and protest. I should add, briefly, that legitimization and protest come into play not only by conferring or denying value to a social reality, but also by making a social reality, and/or by making it known or not known.

The whole question can be summarized thus: an equation between class condition and class consciousness exists when a class succeeds in "seeing" (knowing and evaluating) the whole of social reality from the point of view of its own interest. Cultural domination of one class over another occurs when the latter is forced or induced to see the whole of social reality from the point of view of the interest of the dominating class.

I should add that I tend to interpret the term "class" in a fairly elastic way, and that I realize that it is indispensable to give a definition at least of "interest", as well as to explain what gives a class the power to force another class to accept its own point of view, and what are the ways and the means by which this power is successfully exercised. This is not a theoretical contribution, however, and these few points must serve just as a basis for the correct definition of the area of cultural relationships between the community of emigrants who return to their own country, and public institutions. The criteria we can adopt for the analysis of these relationships have been indicated by the previous analysis and can be expressed by a series of questions:

(1) What are the interests of the emigrants who go back to their own country?

(2) Are the emigrants aware of these interests, or, rather, do they have a vision of reality which is in accordance with and is a function of these interests?

(3) If this is not the case, what are the interests, imposed by which groups or classes, that form the vision of reality of the emigrants?

(4) What expectation do the emigrants have with regard to public institutions?

(5) How does the culture of emigrants lead them to be influenced by institutions? To what degree and in which directions?

(6) Does the culture assumed lead the emigrants to the idea of influencing public institutions? If so, using what instruments and tactics?

(7) Given that of the public institutions the Region is the one which has the best qualified, most relevant and autonomous possibilities for creating a policy for emigrants who return home, how are the problems raised in (4), (5) and (6) dealt with in the relationships between region and emigrants?

Because the analysis of the research data is not yet complete, I can only set out in a summary fashion the tendencies which have emerged so far. These data, which cannot yet be considered definitive, will be presented in the form of answers to the questions set out above. Some quantitative date which have already been analyzed will be used.

## The Region of Puglia: a Search for a Policy which Favours Returning Emigrants

Regarding the interests which characterize migrant workers in general (cf. questions (1) and (2)), it is useful to start with the fact that they are citizens of a country in which it is impossible for them to be workers (i.e. in their own country where the employment structures cannot absorb them), and that they are workers where it is impossible for them to be citizens (i.e. in a foreign country, where they have work, but lack civil rights, command of the language and culture, and the status necessary for participation in society). These migrants are, therefore, always marginal (in addition to the fact that they do not enjoy secure employment, as has already been noted). Thus they never participate effectively in the decisions which touch them. It is in their interest, therefore, to remove one or other of these obstacles, either by getting a job in the place where they are citizens, or by obtaining the citizenship of the country where they are employed.

The studies which have already been made seem to show that returned migrants are aware of their own interests and act in pursuit of those interests only in the sense that they emigrate to acquire abroad the means whereby they may "change" their situation at home. As soon as they have acquired these means, or at least think that they have, they return home.

The change in their situation for which they strive, however, is not to create a stable work situation in their own country. It is instead to create what they refer to as a position of "security". What they mean by this is the ownership of property, most commonly their own house, or a piece of land, both of which secure for them the satisfaction of basic needs: housing and food. When this is achieved, they may put money into a type of investment which, whilst it is secure, is not profitable at all. Eventually they may try to secure themselves an income by renting out part of their house or land.

In order to achieve these objectives, they use the migration period primarily as an opportunity to accumulate savings, since they receive salaries of a European standard whilst at the same time minimizing their consumption to levels even below those which they usually enjoy at home.

The change that these emigrants seek is thus a change in their own personal situation, and not a change in the social system of which they are part. They attempt to do this by entering into possession of property and not be acquiring a job which is secure, skilled and well paid. They seek change through individual action (by accumulating savings through extreme self-denial), and not through collective action (i.e. political and trade union action aimed at modifying the overall pattern of investments, employment, and so on).

This strategy, which has been adopted by many returned emigrants (and will be adopted by the majority of those who return in future) might well be worth encouraging, were it not for the fact that it is effective in appearance only. In reality, it has no effect, in the home country or abroad, on the conditions which actually produce emigration. Whilst these conditions remain unchanged, emigration is inexorably reproduced, sometimes with a gap of a generation, and sometimes for the very same person who, with great self-denial, has built himself a house or bought a bit of land, or a car, but is frequently forced to re-emigrate because these possessions "are enough to prevent one from dying, but not enough to allow one to live". One may conclude, in short, that in pursuing this strategy for change, emigrants do not act in a way which defends their real interests.

With regard to question (3), the migrant work force affects the productive system, as we have already said, because of its mobility — geographical mobility above all, but also mobility from one occupational sector to another, even if generally at the level of unskilled work. The dominant class, taking advantage of an historical fact which is of importance to it, that is to say the connection between horizontal and vertical mobility, *imposes an image of emigration as a change*, or at least as *the opportunity for change*. In this way it achieves a double purpose: by transforming the desperation of the underemployed and unemployed of the marginal areas into hope it blocks their possible explosions of rage, and converts the necessity to leave into a free choice, the "mobilization of mobility".

From the point of view of the social productive system taken as a whole, this desire to change, which pushes the emigrants at a subjective level, can have, however, a double effect. One is positive, in that it makes easier precisely that mobilization of large sections of the labour force whose mobility is necessary if the system is to reproduce itself as such. The other is potentially negative in that there could be a transformation of the demand for a change in individual conditions into a demand for a change in the system as such.

However, there are many elements working to block this process. People believe that they have left as a result of a free choice, and they therefore hold themselves responsible for what happens, even more responsible in that the conditions for improvement exist. More than that, a large objective change has already taken place: there is work, wages are assured, regularly paid and much higher that they were used to in their homeland.

The emigrant, made responsible for his actions and therefore potentially already made guilty for the failures, starts to become aware very early on that this enormous change (work and a wage) does not unleash any other changes: it is not sufficient to work in Germany with a German wage to become "like" a German. Although employed, he is anything but an integrated person: and everybody around reminds him that it is his fault, because it is he who is different.

At this point his own difference has to be accepted. It even becomes necessary, for the reason that only in this way do the inadequacies, failures and the lack of integration cease to be a matter of personal responsibility and became the consequence of an objective fact: "natural", "absolute" and an historical, something that by definition cannot be changed and that therefore has to be accepted as it is. What is more, once this situation has been accepted, it is possible to pursue and attain these ends which would otherwise be unattainable.

The objective fixed by the dominant culture, the possibility of achieving vertical mobility through horizontal mobility, something impossible if pursued in the form of integration into the receiving society, becomes completely realizable as long as they accept their own diversity, and accept also certain means (house ownership) and methods (sacrifices and saving). The possibility that in this way one may seek to realize the desired change, or at least pursue it, is the very thing which make the condition of institutionalized marginality supportable. If within the alien status it is possible to pursue the dominant values, this status becomes stressed in itself: ethnicity, regionalism and local loyalties are set against the racism of the host environment.

The dominant culture in this way constructs the *a priori* of the experience of the subordinate group. Change and diversity become change within one's own diversity, and constitute the cognitive categories and fundamental values within which the emigrant finds himself organizing the facts of his experience. Additionally, and as a consequence, it is the very components of his alien status, the specific forms taken by it, that are the only things he can turn to in order to recognize and evaluate the new experiences offered to him.

The two realities which the emigrant experiences do not become the grounds for a critical judgement; instead, the experience of each hides and impedes understanding of the other.

The emigrant's differences (marginality, lack of recognized skills or mastery of the language) from being an obstacle to integration, which objectively they are, become in the emigrant's mind the necessary condition through which a change in his individual destiny may come about. This change, once obtained, or even if it has simply become obtainable, is the way by which the subject does in fact accept his identification with the social system: the one he started from, the one he has reached, and in the end with both of them.

The interdependence of development and underdevelopment, the structural causes which generate marginality, remain hidden; the two social systems are juxtaposed as though they were independent of each other. In the fragmented understanding of the emigrant, social change as a kind of "give and take", and the circle of cultural domination is closed.

When we try to deepen our understanding of the problems contained in questions (4) and (6), we find ourselves faced with an ambivalent situation. The experiences which they have had abroad seem to have strengthened the generally negative opinion and (traditional) diffidence which Italians have about the institutions of their own country. About 90% of those interviewed during our research claim to have found more justice abroad than in Italy, and about 80% claim to have found more equality abroad than at home. In addition, more than 60% expressed a favourable verdict on the social life of the receiving country: of these some 30% explained that the best thing they found overseas was "order", the lack of clientelism and prevarication, "respect for rights", in a word the honesty of social relations. This firm judgement on a social system in which "rights are respected" is worth underlining for its political relevance. Taken with the verdicts on the equality and justice of the receiving countries it is witness to the emigrants' capacity to appreciate the differences between the two environments. Evidently high-handedness or paternalism in labour relations, clientelistic abuses of power in public offices and the lack of civic sense in daily life are no longer "inevitable" for those we interviewed, but can be criticized, given that they have experienced and appreciated their opposite. It remains to be seen whether the question of how to eliminate them at home will emerge from these criticisms.

Almost all the sample expressed themselves very pessimistically in assessing the situation in their own country, but they also showed political realism and democratic sense. Even if more than 90% of those interviewed consider the Italian situation to be serious, less than 10% attribute this fact to irrational causes and less than 5% propose moralistic or authoritarian solutions. The others attribute specific responsibility to the Italian political classes, and specify particular mistakes in the political economy, and propose realistic solutions.

This is what they say. In practice, however, emigrants do not believe that they can influence the decisions of public institutions. A sizeable minority of them (37%) are members of a trade union, while a much smaller minority are members of a political party, but not even this minority of activists believe that it is possible to influence the decisions of the ruling class very effectively through their organizations.

Relationships in the public arena are conceived of (and practised) as a system of reciprocal but asymmetrical relations between individuals, that is in practice as a hierarchical and clientelistic system, legitimized by an exchange of loyalty against help and protection. Characteristically, each of those interviewed affirmed that "without protectors you cannot do anything", that "you need saints in Paradise", but equally firmly denied that they personally had this kind of protection or had ever used it. I do not believe that this indicates a secretive attitude (*omertà*) but rather a kind of modesty in men who had known and appreciated a more universalistic application of laws and regulations, but do not think they can obtain it in the present situation.

Questions concerned with the specific role of the Regions in relation to emigrants are still being studied by the research group. Analysis is complicated by an obvious factor. The official statute of the Region defines it as a territorial government entity, led by the democratically elected representatives of the citizens. In reality this means a bureaucracy which tends to perpetuate itself and certain powerful groups who tend to assure themselves of control of available resources by means which are not always democratic (Bailey, 1969). Returned migrants have a very weak position in this competition because, as we have seen, they do not manage to organize themselves in groups or to defend their interests by collective action.

The alternative policies which one may devise should obviously be directed towards the achievement of a situation in which the returned migrants are both citizens and workers. Such a situation would constitute the realization of conditions to safeguard their own interests.

As citizens the returned migrants have or could have difficulties of various kinds, and certainly those are different from problems of other citizens. It would be useful, therefore, in order to facilitate their re-integration, to organize or re-organize specialised social or community services, at least in the following sectors: in the social secretariat; in the education service, to give counselling and help to the children of returning migrants, and also to organize, if possible and useful, the further education of adult migrants; in the health service, especially in the areas of occupational medicine and mental health.

As far as the integration of emigrants themselves as citizens is concerned, the role which can be played by those formal organizations which mediate the relations between the individual and society (associations, political parties, cultural groups and so on) is significant, and must be studied. Also important is the role of small groups like the family, kin, neighbourhood, friends, etc.

The re-integration of returned migrants as workers is related to a series of variables of great complexity. From amongst these, four possible policies appear to emerge:

(1) a policy of vocational training and retraining related to the possible future developments of the labour market in Puglia;
(2) a policy of inserting individuals into employment on the basis of their existing qualifications or vocational experience;
(3) a policy of guidance and technical assistance, and financial and fiscal aid to small capital investors who wish to start productive activities in agriculture, crafts, trade or small industries;
(4) a policy of guidance or technical assistance and financial and fiscal aid to those who wish to form cooperatives in order to start productive activities in agriculture, trade, services, crafts and small industries.

In order to carry out these policies the state of the economy in the Region of Puglia is clearly of fundamental importance. Furthermore, in addition to the part played by returned migrants themselves, the role played by the public authorities, the trade unions, and by capital (or better the *"patronat"*) will be a determining factor.

\*    \*    \*    \*

As I said, our research is incomplete. In a further phase we propose to examine in greater depth the conditions under which the suggested policies might be feasible. In this phase the research will take the form of a series of studies of small groups selected on the basis of qualitative criteria. The studies will include:

(1) Analyses of the job opportunities, the possibilities of initiating new productive activities within the present economic structure of the Puglia.

(2) An examination of the bureaucratic and administrative structures of the Region in order to evaluate their capacity to carry out the roles envisaged for them in the various policies we have outlined.

(3) An examination of the trade union, associational and party political structures which (at least according to their constitutions) organize and defend returning migrants, in order to evaluate their capacity to carry out their part of the various suggested policies.

(4) An examination of a group of returning migrants, in order to evaluate their capacity, their propensity and their willingness to adopt such policies. We will study in particular the following variables:

(a) Ideology of change (themes: self-denial, security, material goods, destiny, good luck, whose fault is it?)

(b) Attitudes towards enterpreneurial activities and cooperation (themes: accumulation, investment, risk, competence, organization, functions and division of labour, hierarchy and authority, confidence, etc.).

(c) Attitudes towards trade unions and trade union militancy (themes: exploitation, individual and collective action, corporatism and class solidarity, etc.).

(d) Attitudes to policies (themes: rights and duties, participation and delegation, change within the system, transformation of the system, utopia, power, etc.).

(e) Ideology of "familism" (themes: solidarity, possessiveness, honour, continuity, tradition, etc.).

(f) Ideology of clientage (themes: typology and evaluation of asymmetrical binary relations, the ethic of hierarchical reciprocity, etc.).

For each item one will encourage the respondent to compare his experience in his home country and those which he has had abroad.

In concluding this final phase of the research, we must be able not only to evaluate whether the various policies are both feasible and sound, but we must also be prepared if necessary to propose modifications.

## Note

[1] Parts of this article have been translated from the Italian by Jeff Pratt.

# References

Alberoni, F. and Baglioni, G. (1965). "L'integrazione dell'immigrato nella Società Industriale", Il Mulino, Bologna.

Bailey, F. G. (1969) "Stragagems and Spoils: A Social Anthropology of Politics", Pavilion Press, Oxford.

Barbagallo, F. (1973). "Lavoro ed Esodo nel Sud", Guida, Napoli.

Blumer, G. (1970). "L'Emigrazione Italiana in Europa", Feltrinelli, Milano.

Castles, S. and Kosack, G. (1973). "Immigrant Workers and Class Structures in Western Europe", Oxford University Press, Oxford.

Doxa, (1973). "Indagine sui Lavoratori Italiani all.Estero", Centro di Studi e Ricerche Statistiche, Milano (mimeographed).

Malfatti, E. (1976). "Le migrazioni meridionali alla luce delle statistiche ufficiali. *In* "Studi Emigrazione", Anno XIII, n. 42, giugno 1976.

Marx, K. (1970). "Il Capitale", Editori Riuniti, Roma.

Marx, K. (1971). "Per al Critica dell'Economia Politica", Editori Riuniti, Roma.

Marx, K. and Engels, F. (1972). "L'Ideologia Tedsca", Editori Riuniti, Roma.

Mottura, G. and Pugliese, E. (1975). "Agricoltura, Mezzogiorno e Mercato del Lavoro", Il Mulino, Bologna.

Signorelli, A., Tiriticco, M. C. and Rossi, S. (1977). "Scelte Senza Potere. Il Rientro degli Emigrati nelle Zone d'Esodo", Officina Edizioni, Roma.

# 7

# Communicating with Bureaucracy: The Effects of Perception on Public Participation in Planning[1]

*ROSEMARY LUMB*

During the 1960s it became evident that local government in Britain was no longer fulfilling its role as a democratic means of managing local affairs. Several critical, even despairing, accounts of local councils at that time document the paucity of candidates for election, the non-representativeness of councils in general and the lack of public interest in the activities of local government (e.g. Sharpe, 1962; Rees and Smith, 1964; Green, 1974). The reorganization of local government in 1974 was partly a response to this. At the same time, however, and somewhat paradoxically, members of the public were increasingly willing and able to circumvent bureaucratic processes by organized protest, demonstrations and other tactics which demanded the authorities' attention for their point of view. In response to both these trends, but perhaps particularly the latter, public participation is being introduced into many areas of public life formerly governed by elected representatives alone. The emphasis now given to official forms of participation would seem to imply a recognition on the part of the authorities of the need both to reawaken local interest and to incorporate vociferous protesters into their policy-making procedures.

Planning is perhaps the local government activity which has the greatest impact on the lives of citizens, since it is essentially through the implementation of planning policy that the authorities utilize all resources and provide all services. The introduction of mechanisms for consulting the public before planning decisions are made should, therefore, have signalled a major change in local government procedure. However, since the laws requiring public consultation are left to the interpretation of the individual authorities, it is they who decide how much information shall be given and at what stage and to what extent public opinions will be incorporated into policy. They therefore control the scope and meaning of participation itself. Furthermore, the very institutionalization of the process serves to reduce the impact of public protest — which may or may not have been part of the strategy of formalizing participation procedures in the first place.

There is now a sizeable body of literature on aspects of public participation in planning (e.g. Dennis, 1970; Batley, 1972; Davies, 1972) and most of these studies draw the same adverse conclusions about the process. Official participation is essentially a bureaucratic creation, comprising public meetings, comment forms, meetings with local associations and invitations to write to the planning office. By its nature, therefore, the procedure favours the "middle class", who by virtue of their education, income and experience are better equipped to participate in such ways: these people are articulate, accustomed to dealing with bureaucracy and possess the organizational skills necessary to take advantage of the channels offered. In "working class" areas, by contrast, the population is unlikely to understand the implications of the plans, let alone organize an effective and sustained response. Following from this is the fact that planners tend to adopt different attitudes towards "middle class" and "working class" localities, being more open to suggestions from the former and treating the latter paternalistically; in their approach to slum-dwellers Davies has called planners "evangelistic bureaucrats" (Davies, 1972).

But few of these studies of public participation are anthropological and they tend to stress gross socioeconomic variables and ignore local internal variations (with the notable exception of Simmie, 1971). In three case studies in County Cleveland, however, it was found that socioeconomic factors were not the chief variables in the level of participation. It was also clear that participation in planning was not a process which began with the publication of the Draft Structure Plan and ended with the Examination in Public, but a continuing activity in which past experience was crucial. Thus, public participation is a more complex phenomenon than can be explained by socioeconomic factors alone and requires a diachronic perspective for a full understanding.

In this paper it is argued that public participation in local government procedures depends not upon the mere existence of communication channels, nor even directly on the socioeconomic characteristics of the population concerned, but to a great extent on people's mental images of the system and their perceptions of their place in it. The argument is that people's willingness to participate does not only reflect their ability to understand and use the system effectively, which might well be correlated with education and/or occupational status; instead, it is suggested that public beliefs and attitudes towards local government, planners, and the public participation process itself are more important determinants of levels of participation. Before people will participate they must perceive that they are able to do so effectively and that they will not be merely wasting their time and increasing their frustration with the system. This, therefore, is very much a local-level view of the state and its activities. In attempting this analysis certain "naive assumptions" about complex issues in psychology will be made, but where perception and attitudes form a model for social behaviour this is felt to be justifiable.

The data concern Bridgeham,[2] a small town with a population of about 3000. The town has an old centre and a large council estate, but now functions mainly as a residential area for commuters who live in new, owner-occupied houses. In 1975, 39% of household heads were in professional and managerial occupations, and income and further education levels were correspondingly high. There was an active Parish Council, a Civic Society, two Residents' Associations and many other voluntary organizations in the town, denoting interest in the locality and involvement in its affairs. Yet participation in planning through official channels was not high, nor did it follow the divisions which were clearly evident in the population — either between the professional people and the council tenants, or between the old-established residents and the newcomers. (It should, however, be stated that planning policies affecting Bridgeham in 1975 did not pose any major threat to the community; thus, it may be that there was far greater potential for participation than was manifest at that time.)

The planning authority, whether at County or District level, is a bureaucratic machine and as such its actions are interpreted with all the subjective preconceptions, misapprehensions and generalizations which individuals apply to any bureaucratic structure. Attitudes expressed in Bridgeham varied from "Public participation is absolutely marvellous" to "Public consultation is a mess" (and many, of course, had never heard of it). Such diverse views must radically affect people's responses to the behaviour of the planning authority and their willingness to participate in its activities. But attitudes were not wholly related to socioeconomic status and the data required a more sensitive explanation of attitude formation; for although the majority of active participants were high-income, professional people, a great many respondents with similar socioeconomic characteristics expressed very adverse views of the whole planning process and refused to contemplate participating in it.

No direct questions on perception were asked during the study; all these data derive from various interviews and observations aimed primarily at other information, both factual and attitudinal. There are three main categories of people involved here: eight Parish Councillors, 11 people who wrote letters to the planning office or commented in writing after public meetings (who will be called "letter-writers") and 33 individuals from a random-sample survey whose spontaneous comments cast some light on the imagery in question. The attitudes of non-participants will be examined first and then those of people with varying degrees of involvement.

At the level of least understanding of the system bureaucracy is perceived as a single, undifferentiated body: the whole hierarchy of local government councillors and officers are referred to simply as "them". This generic term seems to imply two dominant conceptualizations of bureaucracy: firstly, its *external* nature and separation from "us", the familiar group, and secondly, the idea that the officers and councillors are a united body in *opposition* to the local community. Warr and Knapper have suggested that "What is perceived derives its meaning from the category in which it is placed and from the way this category is distinguished from other categories" (Warr and Knapper, 1968:7-8). Such categorical imagery clearly influences the local view of the authorities and an example will illustrate its effects. Some years ago a group of local people drew up plans for a social club near the council estate in Bridgeham. The Rural District Council agreed to the site, the North Riding granted planning permission and a brewery was found to finance the club. Then, according to local accounts, the brewery backed out and the site was sold to a private builder. Although four bodies (the County Council, R.D.C., brewery and building company) were involved in these manoeuvres, the whole affair is summed up by people on the estate as "*We* were going to have a social club once, but *they* stopped it". Thus, any unfamiliar body is categorized as external and therefore unfriendly to the local community. The administration is seen as obstructive of local views in another sense too. It not only prevents desired developments, as in the case above, but it is also felt to instigate unwanted changes. This gives rise to such statements as "Why don't they just leave Bridgeham alone?" and "They will develop whether we like it or not". Hence, whether bureaucracy is seen as obstructive or interfering, it is felt to disregard local wishes.

The fact that attitudes are based on stereotyping and generalization from superficial knowledge emerged particularly clearly from questions concerning local government reorganization (by which Bridgeham was moved from Stokesly Rural District in the North Riding of Yorkshire to Stockton District in Cleveland County). Some quotations followed by factual comments will illustrate this point:

> "There are too many amateurs in local government for running a big business like Cleveland County". (In fact, untrained, unpaid councillors have always been the foundation of English local government and the North Riding was certainly no different in this respect.)
>
> "We got on better with Stokesly"/"We don't know who to go to now". (Stokesly is considerably further from Bridgeham than Stockton is; most people do their shopping in Stockton and the Town Hall and planning office are very central.)
>
> "Planners don't care because they're not local people". (In 1975 a County and a District planner lived in Bridgeham, none of the former authority's planners did so.)

To some extent, therefore, such comments reflect the difficulties of reorganization *per se* — people do not yet understand the new system — and the attitudes expressed are based on a comparison between an old and familiar system and a new one still in the process of establishing its identity. This suggestion is supported by the more evident confusion in phrases used by two respondents: "Cleveland District Council" and "the County Council . . . is that Cleveland?" Thus, the structure of the new authority is not yet adequately defined in the local imagery.

These kinds of perception, then, are based on insufficient information and misunderstanding, which are always present to some degree, but have recently been exacerbated by the administrative upheavals. It is evident from the data that such generalized conceptualizations of bureaucracy are most frequently unfavourable; and people with perceptions such as these are unlikely to participate effectively in a public consultation programme, either because they are not sufficiently familiar with the structure to adopt the best strategy, or because their perception of the system leads them to believe that their participation will have no effect on the decision-makers.

Turning to the perceptions of the participators, several of the respondents who had some experience of participation made comments which suggested their attitudes towards the official consultation procedure. Sixteen commented that on the whole public participation was "good"; these were eight Parish Councillors and eight letter-writers. 14 thought the process was "bad" — eleven survey respondents and three letter-writers. And on the public meeting as part of this process, 12 were in favour (eight Parish Councillors and four letter-writers), whilst 15 were against it (ten survey respondents and five letter-writers), the main reason being that the planners were felt to have everything "cut and dried before the meeting"; "*fait accompli*" was another phrase commonly used in this context. Thus, the totals are fairly evenly divided as to the benefits of the participation procedure. The breakdown, however, is interesting: the Parish Councillors were unanimously in favour, the letter-writers were split almost evenly, and the survey respondents were wholly against the participation process. This suggests that there is a close relationship between perceptions of the process and respondents' experience of it. The Parish Councillors were automatically involved in planning consultations, the letter-writers by definition had participated to some extent — though for some a single letter represented the limit of their involvement — and the survey respondents had in general only minimal experience of participation.

This relationship between attitudes and experience of participation seems to be closely related to what Warr and Knapper call "stored stimulus-person information", which they describe as

> "information about the stimulus person which is within the perceiver's memory, being available as the basis of a conceptual judgement. Stored information about what the person has done on other occasions, about what other people have said about him . . ." (Warr and Knapper, 1968:18).

Such stored information creates an expectancy that future behaviour of the stimulus person will be the same as in the past. As suggested above, planning is often seen as something which an external authority imposes on the local population and from past experience it is also frequently associated with development and change. A poster displayed around the town at the time of public consultation had the headline "God and Heaven Save Us from the Planners" and one speaker at a public meeting claimed that "Bridgeham people are

frightened of planning because they are frightened of development",
whilst another called for "natural growth, not plans". This is a basic
misconception which persists even among those who attend public
meetings and write letters: the general image of planning is always of
renewal and development and rarely of its other aspects, conservation
and restrictions on change. "Natural growth" under the North Riding
led to the loss of many old buildings, which the woman who called for
it at the public meeting herself regretted, whereas one of the first
moves of the new authority was to make Bridgeham town centre a
Conservation Area. Responsibility for this misconception lies wholly
with the planners; if they wish to improve their public image in a place
such as Bridgeham they must understand the strength of the stored
information and verbal labelling which associates planning with
development and seek instead to emphasize their function as
conservationists. The Parish Councillors have had dealings with both
the North Riding and Stockton and realize how much more the latter
value old Bridgeham than did the former. It is interesting to note that
the only councillor who preferred the old North Riding was one of the
two District Councillors, who did not rank conservation as a high
priority. Indeed, he sold his Georgian house in the High Street to a
supermarket chain and considered himself lucky to have "got in in
time" — that is, before such developments were prohibited.

The scope of public participation is itself ill-defined by law and also
widely misunderstood. Some people feel that public participation
means only that the planners should allow local opinions to be heard;
if they then see their views being acted upon they will have great
approval for the process. Others presume that they have the right to
tell planners what to do, and if their suggestions are not immediately
adopted they will object to participation *per se*. The data suggest,
however, that the creation of a favourable image of planners as a body
depends more often on the type of contact than on the successful
outcome of any interaction from the individual's point of view. In
general it is those who have had personal dealings with planners who
have the most favourable attitude towards the new authority and its
machinery and such people have not necessarily managed to exert any
influence, as the following case illustrates.

A housewife who organized a petition against further development
on her estate had to fight for the right to be heard at every step and in
the end was able to get only very minor alterations to the plans. Yet she
had a favourable impression of the authority because the process had
allowed her to become involved — to put her opinion to one planner in
his office and to attend a site meeting with planners and councillors.

She thought the planners were "genuinely interested and sympathetic" and "felt that she had been consulted", despite the fact that it was her view that "you have to be alert and insist or you'll be ignored". She was also quite prepared to get involved in a similar way in the future, should the need arise, and did not feel she had wasted her time and effort. Two letter-writers raised the same point of "at least being consulted" when talking about public meetings. This suggests that a very superficial appearance of interest and concern on the part of planners improves their public image vastly and increases the use made of official channels of communication. There are also two important analytical points to be made from this case: first, the influence of episodic judgements on attitude-formation and secondly, the impact of direct as opposed to indirect perception. Again, these are best explained by use of psychological material.

For most people, their experience of dealing with planners is extremely narrow and their attitudes are therefore likely to be based on limited information. Vinacke refers to these conceptual processes as "abstraction" and "generalization" (Vinacke, 1974:152). The individual abstracts a detail from one situation and generalizes his response to any future situation in which that detail occurs. By this method an individual who has even minimal contact with planning or planners will then have a ready-formulated response whenever the contact is renewed. Warr and Knapper, in a discussion of the "expectancy component" of perception, which allows behaviour to be predicted, distinguish between "episodic" and "dispositional" judgements. Episodic judgements are made at the present time on current information, whereas dispositional ones are more permanent attitudes based on past experience and stored information. Furthermore, they suggest that

"Perceivers are extremely willing . . . to translate an episodic judgement into a dispositional one which relates also to other occasions. On the basis of limited information about what a person does in one situation we are prone to attribute to him dispositional characteristics which he is supposed to possess in an almost unrestricted range of situations" (Warr and Knapper, 1968:15).

Clearly, episodic judgements are being used in the public perception of planning. In the case of the woman above, one episodic judgement had created a favourable dispositional judgement: she had been heard by the authorities on one occasion and this led her to expect that the official response would be the same next time. Similarly, an individual involved in an unfavourable episode is likely to expect that any future experience will follow the same lines. Because most people's encounters with planning are infrequent the process is particularly open to perceptions based on single episodes, which may or may not be typical of planners' actions.

Secondly, this case demonstrates the important division between direct and indirect perception in attitude-formation. Direct perception is based on personal contact, whereas indirect perception derives from the intervention of an intermediary — either the media or another person — and the information on which the perception is based is therefore subject to selection and processing by the intermediary concerned. Warr and Knapper provide a useful diagram to express these different types of perception:

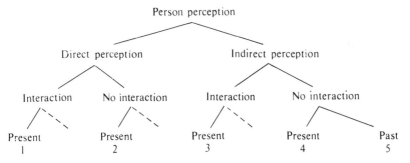

*Types of perception in terms of three characteristics*
*(Warr and Knapper, 1968.) Reprinted with permission*
*of the publisher*

The numbers indicate various perceptual categories, and some examples they give of these are as follows:

(1) Conversations, interviews.
(2) Lectures, ceremonial events.
(3) Telephone conversations.
(4) Live television broadcasts.
(5) Recorded television or radio broadcasts, newspaper reports, verbal accounts.

The relevance of this diagram to the present material is that perceptions of planning fall exactly into these categories. Given that episodic judgements are translated into dispositional judgements, then attitudes can be seen to be formed on the basis of the perceptual incident which had the most impact, or which was most frequently repeated. Those who have had direct dealings with planners, such as the Parish Councillors and the woman in the case cited above, base their judgements on perceptions in Category 1. These perceptions derive from personal interaction and the attitudes were formed at the time of such encounters. The perceptions of those who spoke at public meetings and got an answer fall into the same category, but those who merely listened derive their images from Category 2, in which there was no interaction involved. Some people have telephoned the planning offices and are therefore included in the third perceptual category; others, in Category 4, will have seen live TV broadcasts or heard planners speaking on the radio. But by far the largest perceptual category as far as planning is concerned is the last one. Perception in Category 5 is indirect, involves no interaction and is based on past events. The intervention of an intermediary is at its most influential here, whether it be the press or other people recounting incidents relating to planning. Thus, at this level the information on which judgement is based is the most open to distortion and selection of any which reaches the individual. It is also apparently the perceptual category most likely to produce an unfavourable attitude.

Socioeconomic variables alone, therefore, are insufficient explanation of differential rates of public participation, for even among a population which apparently has all the resources and experience to deal with bureaucrats on their own terms, individuals place more trust in direct, personalized relationships than in the formalized interaction of larger groups or official procedures. Once people are dealing with others as individuals, rather than as bureaucratic bodies, their belief in their own ability to influence decisions greatly increases. Almond and Verba, in a cross-national study of political cultures, found that "When it comes to the support that individuals believe they could enlist in a challenging political situation, they think much more often of enlisting support from the informal face-to-face groups of which they are members than from the formal organizations to which they are affiliated" (Almond and Verba, 1963:192). Thus, although the ability to speak at public meetings and write articulate letters may well be correlated with income, occupation and education, these are not necessarily the main prerequisites of involvement in public participation procedures, which depends to a greater extent on experience than on socioeconomic factors. From the material presented it seems that underneath the diagram an arrow from left to right could be added to represent a favourable/unfavourable continuum in the attitudes manifest towards the planning process. In other words, there is a positive correlation between perception which is direct and based on interaction and a favourable attitude towards the planning process and the propensity to participate.

Throughout the paper the favourable disposition of the Parish Council towards planning has been highlighted — the councillors see public participation as a success, they are aware of the conservation aspects of planning and they prefer the new authority. Reference must therefore be made to the implications of the activities of the Parish Council for public participation in Bridgeham (see Lumb, 1980, for a detailed discussion of the Parish Council). Although not taking part to any great extent in the public participation exercise, the Parish Council has achieved considerable influence over the development of Bridgeham in recent years; yet the statutory powers of a Parish Council are minimal and it has only an advisory role with regard to planning (submitting its views on applications for planning permission to the District Development Committee, as any member of the public can also do). In contrast to the general population, however, the Parish Council benefitted from the continuity of its role during reorganization. The new District authority took pains to present itself well to the Parish Council, through official meetings and other types of contact, and the councillors accepted it as a great improvement. Moreover, from its experience over time and its knowledge of the processes of local government the Parish Council has a high sense of its own political efficacy — that is, it believes itself able to influence decisions which affect Bridgeham. Finally, the Parish Council has had a great deal of direct, personal contact with the planning officials and so developed a favourable attitude towards them. Thus, for several reasons the council knows and is prepared to use the available communication channels (not all of them part of the official consultation machinery) more than any other sector of the population and so is in an advantageous position to make its views heard. It is therefore possible that if the Parish Council were less effective other groups or individuals would emerge and make themselves cognisant of the public participation procedures.

In summary, it seems that although perceptions may be founded on misunderstanding and lack of knowledge or on direct experience and first-hand information, the source of the imagery bears no relation to its durability or potency as a model for action. The majority of the public have had no personal dealings with planners, yet they hold a firm image of them as a body, based on what they read in the papers or hear from others (during the fieldwork it was quite striking what strong — and invariably adverse — reactions were evoked by mention of planning, even from those who proved entirely ignorant of the facts of the local situation). New information is interpreted in the light of the perception already held and usually serves to reinforce it. It seems to require a great deal of contradictory experience for an individual to reclassify his information and alter his original view of planners. But the key variable in successful participation is not the quantity but the quality of communication between the authorities and the public in both directions. Reorganization was an opportunity for the local government hierarchy to present a completely new image of itself and, as seen above, this was successful with the best-informed, the Parish Councillors. Thus, because public participation is controlled by the local authority, those who are best able to participate are the councillors, who have experience in dealing with bureaucracy and interpersonal contact with planners.

There is, of course, a whole area of perception which has not been touched upon here, namely the planners' image of the public. Because those who write letters or speak at public meetings are generally critical, planners tend to see the local population in an equally stereo-typed way as a homogeneous, hostile body. Given this attitude, the planners naturally adopt a defensive stance and participation becomes more like confrontation, alleviated in the case of Bridgeham only by the mediation of the Parish Council. The ideology of the planning profession also perhaps operates to hinder effective public participation, which is seen as an obstruction to the implementation of the plans. And for this reason planners will tend to favour the impersonal and controllable relationships of the public meeting, rather than the face-to-face interpersonal contact which has been described as beneficial to public attitude-formation. The planning authority has no legal obligation to do more than listen to public opinion; but if, as it claims, it really does wish to incorporate local views into its policies, then these stereotyped images on both sides must be broken down by more direct contact to allow effective participation by a wider public than the local councillors.

## Notes

[1] The data on which this paper is based were collected during 1975 for a project supported by the Centre for Environmental Studies at the Department of Anthropology, Durham University; further work in the same area was made possible in 1977 by a grant from the Social Science Research Council.
[2] "Bridgeham" is a pseudonym.

# *References*

Almond, G. A. and Verba, S. (1963). "The Civic Culture", Princeton University Press, Princeton, N.J.

Batley, R. (1972). "An explanation of non-participation in planning", *In* "Policy and Politics", Vol. 1, no. 2, 95-114.

Davies, J. G. (1972). "The Evangelistic Bureaucrat", Tavistock, London.

Dennis, N. (1970). "People and Planning", Faber and Faber, London.

Green, G. (1974). "Politics, local government and the community", *In* "Local Government Studies", 8, June, 5-16.

Lumb, R. (1980). Structural change and brokerage: a Parish Council after reorganization, *Commun. Devel. J.* 15, 2.

Rees, A. and Smith, T. (1964). "Town Councillors, a Study of Barking", Acton Society Trust, London.

Sharpe, L. J. (1962). Elected representatives in local government, *Br. J. Sociol.* XIII, 189-209.

Simmie, J. M. (1971). "Public participation: a case study from Oxfordshire", *In J. Town Planning Institute* 57, no. 4.

Vinacke, W. E. (1974). (2nd edn). "The Psychology of Thinking", McGraw-Hill, New York.

Warr, P. B. and Knapper, C. (1968). "The Perception of People and Events", Wiley, Chichester.

# 8

# The Israel Ports Authority and the Port Workers of Ashdod, Israel

## LEONARD MARS

In his assessment of the Bernstein Research Project in Israel, Emanuel Marx referred to the role of the State in the various constituent studies that comprised that project. He pointed out that the State was not a monolithic giant but was composed of numerous organizations, each internally divided and each with its own personnel, organization and aims (Marx, 1975:136). He also indicated that the Bernstein Project studies revealed the diverse ways in which State bureaucracies interacted with their various and varied clientele. This bureaucratic complexity emerges in one short article that I wrote on the role of the village administrator in an Israeli Cooperative Village (Mars, 1976). There I discussed the way in which that official represented the interests of the Land Settlement Department of the Jewish Agency, which employed him and which administered the village, the political party to which he and the village were affiliated, and the villagers themselves with their manifold economic and political interests. Other studies of villages examined how the Government's agricultural policies affected relationships within villages. The Bernstein Project also studied development towns especially the operation of municipal politics (Aronoff, 1974; Deshen, 1970) and the provision of welfare services (Handelman, 1977; Marx, 1976). These studies, in their different ways, examine the nature of dependence on state organizations, attempts to resist such dependence, and endeavours to exploit that dependent relationship.

This article too is concerned with a development town but one which differs significantly from those studied by Aronoff, Deshen and Marx in that, because of its key economic position in the nation, its dependence on state bureaucracies, national political parties and the *Histadruth* (The General Federation of Labour) is considerably altered. This development town, Ashdod, because of its port and the industry which has been attracted to the port, has prospered and is not a depressed town from which folk seek to escape, on the contrary, its growth has been spectacular since its foundation in 1957.

In this paper I examine relationships between one section of the town's inhabitants, namely the port workers, and their employer, the Israel Ports Authority (I.P.A.), the Union to which they belong, the *Histadruth*, and the Government ministries particularly those of Labour and Transport. The major part of this paper examines the period from 1965, when the port opened, to 1971 when I completed my first fieldwork in Ashdod, but in my conclusion I shall refer to developments between 1971 and 1978 about which further details can be found in Mars (1978b and 1979).

I shall argue that the port workers, or a major section of them, were attempting to gain some degrees of control over their own position in the economy and to resist the control of the I.P.A., the *Histadruth* and the Government, while at the same time having to cooperate with these organizations so that a series of compromises emerged out of this complex interaction, one result of this being a diminution in the power of the I.P.A. and of the local (Ashdod) branch of the *Histadruth*, and a shift in the Government's attitude to port workers.

What cannot be stressed too much is the novelty of the whole social situation, so that what we see is the development of a social system from a variety of different elements. Here we have a new port, administered by a new bureaucracy, in a new town, settled by new immigrants. The interaction of these diverse elements each of which was in the process of growth, and each of which was feeling its way in the new system of relationships resulted in several trials of strength that led to modifications in the division of labour and authority between management and workers, and eventually produced dock leaders of national rather than of local importance whose direct contact with government ministers and senior *Histadruth* officials enabled them to exert strong pressures on their employer, the I.P.A. (Mars, in press).

## The Israel Ports Authority and the Port of Ashdod

The port of Ashdod, which is located 25 miles south of Tel Aviv was opened in November 1965 and its operation resulted in the closing of two of the country's small Mediterranean ports, Jaffa, which had been in operation for at least 3000 years, and Tel Aviv, which had begun operations in 1936. Haifa, hitherto Israel's only large port, situated in the north of the country also felt, though less drastically, the impact of Ashdod's competition, since it suffered an immediate decline in the volume of cargo that it handled.

The first men to be employed as permanent port workers in Ashdod were recruited from two different backgrounds, first from the defunct ports of Tel Aviv and Jaffa, and secondly from the ranks of the labourers who had been employed by the building contractors *Solel Boneh* (the largest construction company in Israel, owned by the *Histadruth*) during the four years that it had taken to construct the port. The original intention of the I.P.A. had been to recruit its labour from the ports of Tel Aviv and Jaffa and to augment this force gradually as Ashdod developed. However, the labourers engaged in the construction of the new port, mainly new immigrants, became concerned about their future employment as the port neared completion and staged a strike in October 1965. Their chief demand was that they be granted employment as dock workers when the port commenced operation. This strike occurred shortly before the general election of 2nd November, 1965 and during a period of economic recession so that there was considerable pressure on the government not only to act promptly, but also to be seen to act promptly. The government quickly responded to the strike and promised that the workers would be transferred from *Solel Boneh* to the I.P.A. This promise compromised the men from Tel Aviv–Jaffa who had already been offered employment in the new port. They were veteran Israelis and experienced port workers who did not see why their livelihood should be jeopardized by new immigrants with no experience of port work. The dilemma facing the I.P.A., that of commencing operations during a trade recession with an excess of labour, was partly resolved by offering severance pay over and above anything hitherto paid to redundant workers. Even so, 319 from Tel Aviv and Jaffa moved south, and 485 *Solel Boneh* labourers joined the I.P.A.

One consequence of this strike was that port workers realized their power to put pressure on their employer, the I.P.A., by virtue of their crucial position in the national economy. Government action signified the submission of port management on what it had regarded hitherto as one of its prerogatives, namely the recruitment of manpower. This submission was reaffirmed in 1967 when workers exerted pressure on the I.P.A., via the government, to accept yet more port workers.

The I.P.A. which is a state-owned corporation was established in 1961 after the Israeli Parliament had passed the Ports Authority Law earlier that year. Although responsible to the Ministry of Transport, the I.P.A. is independent of it in its finances and operations, and is governed by the board of 15 members, eight of whom represent public economic bodies (shipping lines, Export Institute, Citrus Marketing, the *Histadruth*, the Manufacturers' Association and the Haifa Labour Council) and six of whom represent government ministries, presided over by an independent chairman.

According to its statute, the I.P.A. must manage the country's three ports in general (Haifa, Ashdod and Eilat) and each one separately as a viable economic unity, by at least balancing its revenue and expenditure, the latter including development costs, interest and depreciation. Statutory requirements therefore demand that the I.P.A. be a profit-making concern without recourse to government subsidies. Rising costs must therefore be met either by raising tariffs or increased productivity. Higher tariffs are bound to affect the sectional interests of at least some of the members of the board though should they in fact make such a proposal the final decision would have to be ratified by the Government as this is one of the basic issues pertaining to the I.P.A., on which the Government retains the final say (another issue is the I.P.A.'s Development budget). The Government also appoints the members of the I.P.A.'s board and the Director of the I.P.A. and the managers of the various ports.

Hence the same statute that grants the I.P.A. independence also restricts that autonomy by its definition of basic issues which are reserved for the Government. Apart from these statutory limitations on its independence the Authority is also susceptible to the influence and to the policies of the Government and to pressures that groups and organizations can exert on the Government so that in fact the I.P.A. is a government agency. Thus the wider national interests that the Government has to take into consideration may further infringe what senior officials of the Authority regard as their prerogatives. Labour leaders in the ports as well as management are aware of the real *locus* of decision-making in disputes between them. From experience labour leaders know that pressure can be exerted on the I.P.A. by the *Histadruth* and by government ministries, particularly those of Labour and Transport. The I.P.A. and its employees also recognize the power of the *Histadruth* and each has sought its aid in settling disputes in the port of Ashdod and in other ports.

Prior to general elections the power of workers in relation to that of management is enhanced, as was revealed by the strike of the construction workers who built the port. Party politics also affect the relations between management and labour in Israel where government ministries are divided among the political parties that form the ruling coalition. Thus change in the composition of the cabinet can result in a shuffling of ministerial posts among the parties. For example, after the elections of 1969 the Ministry of Transport which since 1948 had been a preserve of *Achdut Avodah*[1] was allocated to *Gahal* a right-wing political party that had first entered the government shortly before the Six Days War in June 1967. The new minister received leading port workers from Ashdod in the home of the mayor of Ashdod, who was also a member of *Gahal*, and subsequently agreed to set up an Inquiry into labour relations in the port of Ashdod. However, by the time the report was published in September 1970 Gahal had already withdrawn from the coalition government and the Ministry of Transport was once again in the hands of the *Achdut Avodah* faction, now a member of the Labour party.

The I.P.A., its employees and the Government are all sensitive to public opinion which each of them attempts to inform and to mobilize in support of its case in dockland disputes. Hence in 1970 the largest Works Committee in the port of Ashdod appointed a local newspaper owner as its public relations advisor in view of the unfavourable publicity that it had incurred as a result of a series of strikes in the port; the Works Committee made this appointment because of what it considered to be the biased statements of the public relations officers employed by the Authority at Head Office and at each of the three ports.

Because of the need for regular consultations between the I.P.A. on the one hand and government ministries, banks, the *Histadruth*, and clients on the other, the headquarters of the I.P.A. were located in Tel Aviv. Proximity to these bodies is indicative of the role of headquarters in relation to its constituents, the three ports. Although each port is independent in its operations and is free to compete with the other ports in attracting clients, headquarters determines development

projects, manpower policy, wage policy, and budgets and therefore
requires close and immediate contact with the institutions especially
governmental, that deal with these matters. Port workers interpret this
location as indicative of the remoteness of the I.P.A. from the daily life
of the ports and perceive the officials in Tel Aviv as bureaucrats who
know little if anything about the waterfront.

## The Town of Ashdod

The town of Ashdod, established in 1956, experienced rapid growth
especially after the decision had been made to construct a deep-water
port there. From a figure of 4600 in 1961 the population rose to 23 300
in 1965, to 38 000 in 1971 and to 52 500 in 1975 (Ministry of Social
Welfare, 1976). Most of this increase was due to immigration,
particularly of new immigrants. Thus in 1965 over half of the
population, 12 000, had immigrated to Israel since 1961. Not only
were the town's inhabitants new immigrants but they were young,
one-half below the age of 19 and two-thirds below the age of 30 years.
Thus Ashdod is a rapidly growing new town populated mainly by
young immigrants and their numerous children.

As the largest single employer in the town, the port and its workers
are of great concern to local politicians who see it as a strong base for
their parties and who also show interest in its affairs. In the national
and local elections held simultaneously in 1969, Ashdod was one of the
several local authorities that split its vote, i.e. voted for one party at
national level and for another at local level (Arian, 1972:103). Nationally
the town voted for the left-wing Alignment, a coalition based on the
Labour parties of *Mapai*, *Achdut Avodah*, *Rafi* and *Mapam*, but
locally it elected *Gahal*, a right-wing alliance between Herut and the
General Zionists (later Liberal) Party. This was the first time in
Ashdod's short history that the labour parties had not controlled the
town and this rejection expressed dissatisfaction with the Alignment on
local issues, among them a dispute between the *Histadruth*, which is
controlled by the Alignment, and the Works Committee of the dockers
of the Port of Ashdod. The fact that the Alignment's candidate for
mayor was also the Head of the Administrative Department of the
Port, which supported the *Histadruth* in the dispute also lost that
party votes.

Although the right-wing *Gahal* gained control of the town council,
nevertheless the Labour parties through their domination of the

Ashdod Labour Council (the local branch of the *Histadruth*) has effective political and economic control over many enterprises in the town. These include those owned or administered by the *Histadruth*. Examples are *Kupat Holim*, the *Histadruth* Sick Fund, which provides medical care to most of the town's residents, and the sports and youth clubs which attract many of the Ashdod's youth. Ashdod port workers sit on the Labour Council as the representatives of political parties. The Labour Council has a department concerned with trade union affairs which has the authority to declare a strike legal, thereby granting official *Histadruth* support to the striking workers. Consequently their roles as port workers and Council members may come into conflict.

The manpower resources of the local branch are limited, consequently one official deals full-time with all the works committees in all the enterprises in Ashdod including the six committees in the Port of Ashdod. Because of the local and national importance of the port, the local official and even his superior, the secretary of the local Labour Council, are often by-passed when disputes occur in the port, since local workers may appeal directly to officials at *Histadruth* H.Q. in Tel Aviv, and to government ministries in Jerusalem.

In short, because of the divided allegiance of its members, its inadequate manpower resources, and the strategic national importance of the port leading to the direct involvement of national bodies, the local Labour Council is weaker than its nominal inferior, the local committee of dock workers.

## The Growth of the Port

Ashdod port expanded rapidly during the first years of its operation and this expansion was significant not only for its own workers but also for employees in Israel's other Mediterranean port, Haifa, which competes for cargoes with Ashdod. The initial effect of Ashdod's opening in Haifa was that the latter suffered a decline in the handling of both exports and imports as some of these moved to its young rival. Thus it was not until 1969–70 that Haifa exceeded the amount of cargo that it handled in 1965–66.

The opening of Ashdod port not only affected Haifa economically but also diminished the political power of Haifa port workers. Because Tel Aviv and Jaffa were lighterage ports and only handled a few ships per month, Haifa's dockers did not fear their competition and did not need an alliance with their workers. However, the new port was a serious rival and when the Haifa men went on strike after Ashdod had commenced operations, they appealed to the Ashdod workers not to accept ships diverted from Haifa.

One outcome of rapid expansion and subsequent opportunities for promotion was that expectations of advancement in the work-place became to be considered the norm and this led to disappointment by 1971 when workers who had been employed perhaps six months or a year less than their workmates felt their promotion prospects to be blocked. Promotion was not confined to rank and file workers, since their elected leaders, members of the Operation Workers' Committee, also benefited and became foremen. Thus three predecessors of the current Secretary of the Workers' Committee of the Operation Department gained promotion between 1965 and 1967 as did other members of that Committee. Changes in the membership of the Operations Workers' Committee affected relationships between the Committee and the port management, especially when one committee refused to acknowledge agreements reached by its predecessor. Managerial positions also expanded with the growth of the port and new posts were created which were filled by men with limited administrative experience.

Thus rapid expansion created a situation of fluidity both within the ranks of the workers and in their relationships with management. As far as management was concerned, the turnover in leadership among port workers created problems about continuity and predictability in relationships so that management itself became interested in the establishment and maintenance of a stable leadership for port workers.

The port of Ashdod is divided into five departments (see Table 1).

*TABLE 1: Permanent employees in Ashdod Port per department as on 31 March 1970*

| Administrative | Engineering | Finance | Marine | Operations | Total |
|---|---|---|---|---|---|
| 52 | 97 | 74 | 111 | 1167 | 1501 |

Source: Year Book of Israel Ports Statistics 1969-70.

By far the largest is the Operations Department whose main task is the loading, unloading and storage of cargo. Space precludes a long description of the occupational complexities of this department (cf. Mars, in press) suffice is to say that the basic work unit is the gang of stevedores, assisted by winchmen or coastal crane operators and by forklift truck operators whose work is coordinated by the gang leader, known as the signaller, all of whom are supervised by a foreman.

The gang is not a stable unit since its composition may be modified by technological factors, e.g. the type of crane employed, by the nature of the cargo that is worked, which may require more or less workers, and by workers' norms, e.g. the principle of seniority which is critically relevant when work is scarce so that junior signallers may have to stand down and their gangs be dispersed (Mars, in press).

The basic cause of fluctuation in the composition of the work gang is the seasonal flow of work. The permanent work force is sufficient to man 45 work gangs per day; at the height of the citrus season between 65 and 67 gangs are required.[2] This total is achieved by the recruitment of temporary labourers from the labour exchanges in and around Ashdod. At this time winchmen become signallers, and stevedores with winchmen's certificates move up on deck and in turn are replaced in the hold by temporary unskilled workers.

The Operations Department is characterized by its dominance within the port, by the transience of its basic unit, by the high degree of segmentation among the department's workers which derives from the diversity of occupations. Thus the department contains three separate works committees, one for foremen, one for warehousemen, and one for the men who work in gangs assisted by the crane and forklift operators. This last committee, which is styled the Operations Committee, itself represents a wide range of occupations.

Against this background of transient working relationships there is one stable fixture, the Operations Committee, to which the dockers can turn when they have problems whether about pay, conditions of employment, promotion, and, in some cases, domestic problems. The position and strength of the Operations Committee in the port which arises out of the segmentation of its workers, is enhanced by the status which management accords it in dealing with those workers and their problems.

Management has acquiesced to the incorporation of the Operations Committee into the administrative organization of the port. This incorporation, however, was not granted to the Committee as an automatic right but was achieved as a result of a series of confrontations between management and workers, as a result of which management lost what it considered to be some of its prerogatives, such as complete control over the recruitment of labour, control over the promotion of workers and of managerial officials, and control over the timing and holding of occupational courses. Outwardly and officially, management preserves a front that it does still have the decisive say in these matters, but privately it is aware that things are not what they were nor what it officially holds them to be. The Committee is content to maintain this front since it enables it to hold power without being publicly responsible for the administration of the department or of the port.

The first major confrontation between management and the workers in the Operations Department took place in December 1966 and early in 1967, a period of economic recession in Israel when there was little work in the port. This confrontation was known as the Strike of the Forty and its origins are to be found in the agreement to transfer labourers engaged in construction of the port from *Solel Boneh* to the employment of the Authority which was signed by the latter and the *Histadruth*. This agreement stipulated that those who had been in employment with the constructor on, and prior to 31 December 1963 would have the right of transfer. (There were labourers who had commenced work after that date but before the port was officially opened in November 1965.) Among them were the 40 labourers who staged a hunger strike in the offices of the Ashdod Labour Council and outside the gates of the port.

The 40 had been employed as temporary port workers since the opening of the port and had been given the impression by the Works Committee that they too would be granted permanent status despite the fact that they were clearly excluded by the terms of the agreement. The local Labour Council after initially opposing the 40 decided to give them backing. The permanent workers were divided on the issue; those who subscribed to the view that the legal agreement should be honoured were over-ruled by more militant men, some of whom came from the rank and file, among them the current Secretary of the Works Committee, who decided to back the demands of the 40.

After progressing through the various stages for settling disputes management and workers and their representatives in the Labour Council, and in the Trade Union Department of the *Histadruth*, agreed to submit the question to the arbitration of the Minister of Labour.

Management based their case on two points:

(1) that the 40 were not covered by the transfer department;
(2) that the Minister of Labour had stated in the *Knesset* (the Israeli Parliament) that an enterprise would not be obliged to accept more workers than were economically required for its operation. Management argued that the recruitment of manpower was its prerogative and that management alone would determine along rational, economic lines the labour force it required; moreover,

during the recession there was not enough work for the permanent workers, let alone for another 40, the equivalent of more than two work gangs.

The Works Committee and the *Histadruth* conceded that management was legally right to exclude the 40 from permanent employment but they stressed the role of the port in the economy of the new town of Ashdod and argued that management should absorb the men in order to establish good will with the town during the recession; they also argued that the port would eventually require additional manpower.

The Minister of Labour in his arbitration found that the Authority was right to deny the 40 permanent employment, but argued that the port of Ashdod was an expanding concern and therefore it should grant the 40 the status of "minimum workers", i.e. a transitional status between temporary and permanent workers which guaranteed the worker a minimum number of days work per month gradually increasing over a period of years until he became a full-time employee. (This status was abolished in 1969.)

As a result of this verdict, the port manager of Ashdod resigned on the grounds that his position had become untenable. Port management considered that the verdict had encouraged workers to repudiate signed agreements and to use force to back up their demands in the knowledge that the Government and the *Histadruth* would give them support.

The Government, however, took into consideration factors that were outside the scope of port management such as the social, economic and political problems of development towns populated by new immigrants during a period of recession. Since the port was a part of the public sector of the economy it was possible for the Government to press workers into that sector over which it had power rather than into the private sector wherein it was impotent.

The strike leaders, who regarded the verdict as the triumph of natural justice over a narrow, legalistic attitude of management, appreciated that they had to rely on their own efforts rather than those of the *Histadruth* which had signed the original agreement. The dispute heralded the arrival of leaders whose strength derived not from links with the *Histadruth* nor with the political parties, but from within the port itself. However, the emergence of such leaders meant that they were courted by political parties and by the *Histadruth*.

The strike was successful because the Committee was able to mobilize forces, particularly governmental, that lay outside of the port, but which could be invoked legitimately as part of the accepted procedure for dispute settlement. Another confrontation a few months later, which concerned the recruitment of foremen from outside the port, did not have as successful a solution as the Committee had wished but paved the way for the Committee to insist that it would, in the future, never accept candidates for the post of foreman from outside the Operations Department and *a fortiori* from outside the ports even though the Labour Agreement stipulates that posts within the Authority are open to all of its employees.

The I.P.A. is thus caught between the demands of government ministries and between the pressures exerted by its employees. Thus, after pressure from workers the I.P.A. relinquished control over areas that could be defined as non-work, such as the allocation of the canteen licence, and the management of a minor insurance fund, since these concessions could be considered not to be challenges to its managerial position. On the recruitment of labour the I.P.A. was legally bound to accept the arbitration of the Minister of Labour, who saw the issue as one that reached beyond the confines of the port to embrace the social and economic welfare of new towns inhabited by new immigrants. In this instance the pressure on the I.P.A. which had originally come from below, from its workers, was strengthened from above by the government. However, the I.P.A. under its first Director, a tough, capable, and independently minded person, so frequently came into conflict with the government, the *Histadruth* and with the dockers, that in 1970 the Director was ousted from his post after an inter-ministerial Committee of Inquiry on Labour Relations in the port of Ashdod, and was replaced by a man from the Foreign Office whom the government hoped would be more susceptible to its influence.

The dockers are able to exert pressure on the government because of the vital economic and political role of the port in the national economy. Unlike some other workers in the port, for example the administrative, engineering, and warehouse employees, the dockers can bring the port to an immediate standstill by their refusal to work. A stoppage in the port is not simply a local event; rather it is a national concern in a small country with two main ports which constitute its lifelines. Because of its national significance government ministers and senior officials of the *Histadruth* quickly become involved in labour disputes in the port. The leaders of the dockers, who have direct contact with such notables, themselves become national figures who owe their position to the local power-base that they have built up in the port quite independently of political parties or of the local Labour Council. This power, moreover, was derived from a series of industrial conflicts which challenged the claims of the I.P.A. to jurisdiction in matters of recruitment, promotion and technological change.

In this conclusion I consider two problems that arise from the material that I have presented:

1. the impact of the state of the nation's economy on the dock-workers and their leaders;
2. the alternation between bureaucratic and more personalized forms of organization (*protktsia*) among portworkers' leaders which requires some discussion of changes in the period since 1971.

1. A boom or a recession in the economy of the nation has obvious and immediate repercussions on the earnings of port workers, on their relations with their employers, the I.P.A. and on their relations with government ministries. National economic fluctuations are of grave concern to the leaders of the dockers not only because their workers lose money but because their own positions are threatened.

First, a brief comment about the earnings of dockworkers, which is based on an incentive or productivity scheme. Dockers receive a low basic wage which is supplemented by bonuses when output exceeds an agreed norm. When no work is available then men receive only their basic pay. Earnings vary seasonally: in the winter months (November–April) when citrus is exported, wages rise, but they fall again during the slack summer months. However, if the country's volume of trade increases work becomes available in the summer and consequently dockers enjoy more pay; if a national recession develops then dockers become unemployed and receive their basic rate. When national and hence local prosperity is enjoyed then dockers are satisfied with their leaders (moreover the time is not opportune for dissatisfaction to take the form of opposition) but during a recession they exert pressure on them and disgruntled rank and file men may emerge as leaders, as happened in the Strike of the Forty, when the established leaders who had signed the original agreement, and were therefore legally bound to honour their signatures, were repudiated by men from the shop floor. However, the overthrow of established leaders during a recession may be achieved by another group of workers as happened in 1976–77, when an occupational elite composed of training instructors spearheaded the downfall of the Committee (Mars, 1979).

During a recession the attention of government ministries is drawn by workers to the situation in the ports — this attention may be expressed by *Histadruth* officials on behalf of the nation's labour force or by local portworkers' leaders on behalf of their constituents' anxieties. Either way government involvement is procured and national socioeconomic considerations, as we have seen, over-ride local issues between management and workers. During the citrus season when the port is fully occupied, grievances between workers and management, or between workers and government over pay policy, may involve strike action on the part of workers in pursuit of their claims since this is the period when they can exert maximum pressure on the other party to the dispute. As in a recession these local strikes during the citrus season rapidly become national issues which result in the direct involvement of various government ministries and also attract the attention of the media and of public opinion.

2. During the first four years of the port's existence we have seen that there were several major conflicts between the I.P.A. and its workers over issues of recruitment, promotion, conditions of work and also on matters that I have not discussed, especially the key question of the incentive payment scheme about how output norms were to be determined. The outcome of these disputes was that the Shop Stewards' Committee triumphed and the I.P.A. conceded (Mars, in press). During this period of expansion there was a continuous turnover in personnel on the Committee since several shop stewards were promoted to the ranks of foremen. This unstable leadership caused difficulties for the I.P.A. which became interested in establishing a more permanent body of dockworkers' leaders. These leaders were those who had risen from the rank and file during the Strike of the Forty to become Committee members and whose success in conflict had resulted in the bestowing of legitimacy on them by workers. Following the bestowal of legitimacy by workers, management too bestowed its own legitimacy on that Committee and incorporated it into the administration of the port (Mars, in press).

Having gained office in 1969 the Committee consolidated its position, but with the passage of time became corrupt, bestowing favours on its supporters and penalizing its opponents in the manner of a patron (Mars, 1979). Since members of the Committee had become full-time, white-collar functionaries remote from the waterfront, earning much more than ordinary workers, and socializing outside the port with senior management it became suspect in the eyes of the rank and file. When trade declined in 1975–76, especially in Ashdod,[3] the time became ripe for the emergence of an opposition which subsequently overthrew the personalized regime of its predecessor (Mars, in press and 1978b).

This new Committee whose leaders were the instructors from the Port's Training School was more bureaucratically orientated than its predecessor and its election had repercussions throughout the port. Thus senior port managers who had enjoyed personal ties both inside and outside the port with members of the previous Committee found themselves in an unfamiliar situation when confronted by a Committee imbued with an ethos more formally bureaucratic than that to which they subscribed themselves. Hence in 1977 the port manager was replaced and in 1978 his deputy was eased out of his job and transferred to Head Office. Whereas senior managers of the port regretted the overthrow of the charismatically led Committee, middle-level managers welcomed its downfall and the arrival of a Committee dedicated to maintaining the formal rules pertaining to punctuality, discipline and honesty.

Among the changes introduced by the new Committee were the following; all but four of the eleven Committee members were to return to full-time dock work; the allocation of work on a more equitable basis so that there was not such a disparity between the earnings of senior and junior men; the hiring of Israel's top labour lawyer to scrutinize documents presented to the Committee by management. Although the new Committee was more bureaucratically inclined than its predecessor its supporters were not, and they expected it to bestow patronage and reward them in the manner that the previous Committee had rewarded its own faithful followers, and in this they were disappointed.

The new Committee assumed office during a period when the port's trade was in decline, part of a national and indeed international recession, which the Committee could do little to alleviate though it did agree to the opening of the new Container Terminal which the previous Committee had refused to operate for 18 months, in order to be able to compete with Haifa Port on equal basis. No sooner had the new Committee been installed that it found itself involved in negotiating a new Labour Contract. One of its main aims was to improve the basic rate of pay but it failed to realize this goal since management adopted a tough position, which it could afford to maintain during a recession.

In March 1978 on a brief visit to Ashdod Port I learned that the new Committee itself had been ousted a few months earlier by a combination of forces based on the deputy port m   ger (his parting shot before leaving the port), the holder of the port portfolio in the local Labour Council, who subsequently lost his job, and by a member of the Committee who had defected and had rejoined the charismatic former Secretary, together with some rank and file who had remained loyal to that Secretary and other rank and file who had not received the patronage that they had expected for supporting his overthrowers, and most importantly because members of that new Committee had refused to campaign with the new Secretary since they objected to his increasing personal rule, who though he had not so intended, had begun to adopt his predecessor's personal style of rule.

The material presented has been complex involving persons, factions groups, trade unions, political parties, local and national institutions, engaged with each other in part or in whole at different levels in a variety of combinations in diverse situations. However, if we focus on the systematic features of the data we can see some regularity — a constant oscillation between a system which combines both patronage and bureaucracy but which swings from one pole to the other. These swings are attributable to the fact that neither managers nor workers are homogeneous groups of men; each contains segments that adhere to the ideas and practices of bureaucracy and patronage; consequently alliances develop between relevant segments of the two parties. Workers have been incorporated into the administration of the port on a *de facto* basis — they have consequently adopted various bureaucratic practices but at the same time their leaders are seen as patrons by their constituents and occasionally act as such. When the time is ripe for opposition then their patronage is attacked and their opponents stress the bureaucratic ethos, but once in office attempts to act bureaucratically are thwarted by supporters who expect patronage in return for their earlier support and who are prepared to switch allegiance if they go unrewarded, as needs they must during a recession, so that the cyclical process continues as before.

## Acknowledgements

The research was carried out in 1970–71 under the direction of the late Professor Max Gluckman of the University of Manchester on Research Grant 779/1 of the Social Science Research Council of Great Britain. In the summer of 1977 a further grant HR 5209 from the SSRC enabled me to pursue a limited follow-up study. I should like to point out here that this research benefited from my earlier work in Israel which was financed by the Bernstein Israel Research Fund whose trustees I wish to thank. Part of this paper has been published under the title of "Politics and Administration in the Israeli Port of Ashdod" in the *Institute of Development Studies Bulletin* **9**, 33–38 (February 1978), (Mars, 1978a).

## Notes

[1] *Achdut Avodah* — a left-wing party which in 1965 was a member of the Alignment with *Mapai* and which in 1969 was a constituent founder of the Israel Labour Party with *Rafi* and *Mapai*.
[2] These figures apply to the period 1970–71; subsequent technological and organizational changes have reduced these numbers and have resulted in the cessation of the recruitment of temporary labourers.
[3] Ashdod declined by 21.2%; Haifa by 6.5%. In fact Ashdod's tonnage for 1975–76 (3052 million tons) was its lowest total since 1971–72 (2983 million tons) a situation exacerbated by the growth in the labour force over that period. Source: Annual Report of the I.P.A. 1975–76.

## References

Arian, A. (Ed.), (1972). "The Elections in Israel 1969", Jerusalem Academic Press, Jerusalem.

Aronoff, M. (1974). "Frontiertown: The Politics of Community Building", Manchester University Press, Manchester.

Deshen, S. (1970). "Immigrant Voters in Israel", Manchester University Press, Manchester.

Handelman, D. (1977). "Encounters Among the Aged: The Social Organization of Interaction in a Jerusalem Setting", Van Forcum, Amsterdam.

Israel Ports Authority (1969–70). Year Book of Israel Ports Statistics 1969–70; Annual Report 1969–70; Tel Aviv.

Mars, L. (1976). The position of the administrator in an Israeli cooperative village. *Sociologica Ruralis* **16**, 41-55.

Mars, L. (1978a). Politics and administration in the Israeli port of Ashdod, *Institute Devel. Studies Bull.* **9**, 33-38.

Mars, L. (1978b). Report to the SSRC on Grant No. HR5209 entitled "'Shifts in Political Leadership Among Israeli Dock Workers in Ashdod Port", available from British Lending Library, Boston Spa, Lincolnshire.

Mars, L. (1979). Learning the ropes: the politics of dockland. *In "The Anthropology of Work"*, (Ed. S. Wallman), Academic Press, London, and New York.

Mars, L. (1980). Leadership and Power Among Ashdod Port Workers. *In* "A Composite Portrait of Israel", (Ed. E. Marx), Academic Press, London and New York.

Marx, E. (1975). Anthropological studies in a centralised State: the Bernstein research project in Israel. *Jewish J. Sociol.* 17, 131-150.

Marx, E. (1976). "The Social Context of Violent Behaviour", Routledge and Kegan Paul, London.

Ministry of Social Welfare, Israel (1976). Social Profile of Settlements in Israel (in Hebrew), Jerusalem.

# 9

# Buying a Share: State Institutions and Local Communities on the Periphery — A Case from Shetland

REGINALD BYRON

The anthropologist working in Europe who takes a community as his object of study is soon confronted by the fact that he can study his community only in a relative sense. "Community" usually conveys to anthropologists some notion of residential and cultural integrity: a place where people live and work in a largely inward-looking field of social relationships that is bounded by geographical, economic, political or social differences with the world outside. In Europe, one of the anthropologist's particular difficulties is in knowing by what criteria his community is bounded and where the boundaries should be drawn, in other words, in what sense it can be said to have "integrity". No anthropologist working in contemporary Europe can fail to be aware that his community is in a very direct and immediate way part of wider *milieux*, that these wider *milieux* affect the things that happen in his community, and that the relation between his community and the world outside is a continuously changing one. An outstanding example of this is the changing character of the relation between local communities and state institutions, and the increasing dependency and clientship of local communities that has resulted from the gradual growth and centralization of the powers of governmental bureaucracies (Boissevain, 1975:12). Thus the anthropologist who wishes to take a long view in explaining why the people in his community think and behave as they do is inevitably led beyond its boundaries. It is here that a very thorny problem arises: how does the anthropologist identify these external factors and influences, evaluate their status as evidence, and accommodate them in his account of social reality?

This essay will seek to explore one possible approach to this problem — the concept of centre–periphery relations. To the anthropologist, the attractiveness of the centre–periphery idea is that it appears to enable one to work out the levels and relations of economic, political and cultural hegemony that exist between any two or more given structures. Thus one can identify central and peripheral groups and processes within a village: or analyse the centrality of a village in relation to its hinterland; or the peripherality of a village in relation to a nearby town, the national capital, international corporations, and so on. Chains of relations can be identified not only between local communities and larger structures, but also between nations and regions; even a "world-system" has been delineated in these terms (Wallerstein, 1974). One ingredient of centre–periphery relations which has come to be regarded as diacritical is the notion of "transfer payments". In the following case material, I shall attempt to show how a change in the system of transfer payments has affected the social organization of fishing in the Shetland community of Burra Isle.

Let me first make clear what is meant by "transfer payments". Transfer payments are sums of money in one form or another that the centre allocates to the periphery. There are many reasons why a centre might wish to do this: in the European context it is usually said to subsidize marginal employment or surplus population. In Europe, these transfer payments take the form of state pensions, disability and unemployment compensation. Although in most countries all citizens qualify for such benefits, whether or not they live in the periphery, in practice the age- and employment-structure of most peripheral areas mean that the amounts actually transferred are disproportionately high *per capita*. Transfer payments also frequently include special concessions not ordinarily available to other citizens and localities, such as agricultural subsidies, grants and loans to local producers, subsidized transport, housing, communications, educational and medical services in outlying areas, and so on. Common Market regional policy, for example, is essentially a package of concepts about what economic and social responsibilities the centre accepts in relation to its periphery. These concepts are articulated largely through transfer payments. National governments have parallel policies. In Europe, the amounts of money transferred to peripheral areas have increased dramatically in the last 30 years.

To ask questions about transfer payments and their effects on the local level in the European setting seems especially appropriate if only because few, if any, local communities in Europe are autonomous or self-sufficient to the degree that one can still readily find in Third World countries. A highly developed system of transfer payments on a comparatively large scale may indeed be a characteristic feature of the relationship of central state institutions and local communities on the periphery in Europe.

The Shetland case material that I shall describe concerns the capitalization of fishing: the buying of boats and equipment it is necessary to have to set up shop as a fisherman. This is an area in which central government agencies are now heavily involved, but this was not always so. Before 1945, there were no state credit schemes for fishermen.

Up to the Second World War, most of the equipment the fishermen needed they made themselves. Boats were built by part-time shipwrights in Burra, and old sailing boats were acquired second-hand from the Buchan coast of Scotland and rebuilt as motorboats. The long lines and small lines for halibut, cod and haddock were made from hemp and cotton cord and twine, re-using old hooks. Virtually any old boat that could move under its own power, and a few sets of lines were all that was needed. A complete outfit of fishing equipment could be obtained for a capital outlay of betwen two and four hundred pounds, for an ordinary haddock motorboat. The crew of a haddock boat was four men, who shared the expenses and profits equally: the investment of any single shareholder probably never was more than £100, and was usually a good deal less — say £60-70. This was just about the amount of money a fisherman might expect to clear as profit on his share at the end of a moderately good season. But since not all seasons are good seasons, he could not reasonably expect his share to pay for itself in a single year, but he could expect it to do so in two or three years. As well as the haddock boats, other kinds of boats and equipment were also used: two-man mussel dredgers, rowboats requiring an outlay of £10-25; and herring drifters, motor boats that were used only during the summer season and carried a crew of hired men in addition to the four shareholders who actually owned the boat. A herring drifter cost about the same as a haddock boat, but if one joined the crew as a hired man, no initial outlay was necessary.

In order to acquire the £60 or £70 it cost to buy a share in a fishing boat, we might hypothesize something like this: a 16-year-old takes a job for a wage on a summer herring drifter for three summers and manages to save £15 of his wages. He invests this in a mussel dredger which he uses during the winter season, selling his catch to the haddock fishermen, who use mussels as a bait for their lines. He continues to work as a hired man on a drifter in the summers. Eventually he accumulates £50 in savings and sells his share of the dredger for £15. He now has £65 to invest in a haddock boat, which provides a more stable income than a drifter. Drift-net fishing however, has the possibility of a big pay-off. A few good catches during the course of a season could make the difference between scraping along and having money to spend. Most haddock fishermen, for this reason, put some of their profits from haddock fishing toward the cost of a share in a drifter, alternating boats and gear with the season.

There were three other ways of getting the money to buy a share. The first was to ask for an advance from a merchant. The merchants most likely to agree to loans were, not surprisingly, fish merchants who, in lieu of asking for interest, usually made it a condition of the loan that the catch be sold to them alone. In general, this way of getting the money was least preferred, as it compounded the fishermen's already dependent relationship.

A second and more preferred way of getting the money was to take up a vacancy in an existing partnership and to "work off" one's share, forgoing any claim to the profits until the other partners had reclaimed the cost of the share. Thereafter, one was entitled to a full and equal proportion of the profits.

A third alternative was to go sailing in the merchant navy until enough of one's wages were saved to return home and buy a share. This solution was often preferred, as it was the only one of the three alternative ways of getting the money that did not involve accepting a dependent relationship as a debtor.

However the money was got, a fisherman during the inter-war years could expect to be a shareholder in a haddock boat by the age of 25 or 26 and, if he wished, a shareholder in a drifter soon after. Once this rather modest plateau of capital investment was reached, a fisherman was "set up" for the rest of his working life. The Burra fishery was neither highly capital intensive, nor was capital the major constraint in its development.

Instead, fishing was highly labour intensive, involving not only the fishermen themselves, but also their families as well. Nearly every able-bodied person in Burra contributed his labour in some way during some part of the year. Old men and boys supplied mussels, mended gear and cleared lines. Girls and women spent up to nine hours a day baiting each man's share of 1800 hooks. During the summer herring season, the girls and women worked on the herring stations for the merchants, gutting, salting and packing the fish for export. The old men mended the nets and the boys were either given jobs on the drifters or worked on the herring stations. The need for labour went beyond the boundaries of the community. During the herring season, Burra was one of the major employers in Shetland; between 40 and 60 men from other parts of Shetland were regularly hired to top up the ten-man crews of the drift-net boats, and at one stage young women were recruited in the Western Isles to work on the herring stations in Burra.

Getting enough people to do all the jobs was a perennial problem. There was little scope for highly selective criteria of recruitment to work groups. Fishing crews tended to be *ad hoc*, loose associations of neighbours, friends and kinsmen. The Burra fishery expanded slowly but steadily through the 1930s, absorbing a continuous trickle of immigrants from other parts of Shetland who settled permanently in Burra and were taken into Burra crews. During the war years, however, important changes began to take place. Fish prices paid to fishermen rose greatly, while the plentiful supply of cheap labour, upon which line fishing depended, became a thing of the past. These wartime profits were invested in new technology to compensate for the shortage of labour. The adoption of seine nets dispensed with hooks, lines, bait and the tedious preparation associated with line fishing. By the war's end, there were many fewer fishing jobs, and those that remained were much more highly capitalized.

The growing amounts of money invested in fishing equipment during the war years made the control of capital crucially important. Recruitment to fishing teams became more selective and their composition more stable. In the relatively small number of cases where it was possible, fishing capital was kept "in the family" and close kinsmen were chosen as fishing partners. The ethic of kinship buttressed joint ownership. Fathers and sons and brothers pooled their profits and savings in a continuous process of trading up from old boats and equipment to newer and more profitable boats and gear (cf. Lofgren, 1972 and Wadel, 1972).

From 1945, which marked the introduction of state credit schemes to rebuild Britain's fisheries by financing the purchase of new, purpose-built boats, this tendency towards the formation of family partnerships was greatly exacerbated. A crucial threshold had been reached. A new post-war boat cost about £12 500 ready for sea.

Although the government provided 85% aid (between 15–25% in an outright grant and the rest in a loan) this still left a balance of about £2000. One response to this was to add a fifth man to the traditional four partners, spreading the burden a bit more thinly. Even so, each man had to come up with about £400, an increase of more than 500% over the cost of a share in pre-war days. The second response to this was that over the ensuing decade, the family partnership became the predominant ownership structure.

By the late 1960s, a new boat cost £30 000, and by the early 1970s would cost £60 000 or more. Although the 85% aid still held, the cost of a share was now at least £1500, and up to £3000. Fishing was now highly capital intensive, and a clear separation had emerged between the family partnerships, who owned the newest and best boats, and the dwindling number of non-family partnerships, who owned the older, smaller and less profitable boats. The partners in these latter boats consistently failed, because their earnings were low, to recruit the young, highly motivated and skilled men they needed to improve their economic situation: they were caught in a vicious circle and stayed at the bottom of the heap. The family partnerships, in contrast, could afford to be selective in choosing their hired men (each boat normally carried three, in addition to the five partners). From the hired man's point of view, a job on a family boat gave better prospects of higher earnings, which might be saved up to buy a share of his own, in partnership with his brothers or cousins. From his employers' point of view, however, it was preferred to recruit their own sons and nephews, when they were available, over whom they could exercise powerful social sanctions to ensure their contribution to the family enterprise. As far as the employers were concerned, money given to a non-kinsman was money thrown away.

By the late 1960s, the main means by which fishing capital was transferred in Burra was through family patrimonies. A patrimony was the most common and direct way that a young fisherman got his start as a shareholder in a boat. Economic strata based on a differential access to capital were clearly emerging as a direct consequence of this. Young men whose families did not own boats had rapidly diminishing chances of jumping the queue of shareholders' sons.

In 1970, the Highlands and Islands Development Board, a Scottish regional agency, began a scheme intended to help revitalize fishing in areas where it was declining, principally in places like the Western Isles, Orkney and parts of Shetland, where there were few other sources of employment. The scheme provided for a grant and loan to cover the down payments that remained after other government aid had been granted on a new or second-hand boat and gear. By this means it was hoped to eliminate the steeply rising first threshold to boat ownership that was threatening the continuity of fishing, and therefore of employment, in many rural communities (although Burra, with virtually full employment and by comparison very prosperous, was certainly not one of the communities the Highlands Board had in mind). The scheme was made available to all inshore fishermen in the Western Isles, Orkney and Shetland. The normal qualifications for aid from the scheme were six months' experience as a fisherman, two letters of reference (one from a skipper), and an age of 18 or over.

In Burra, the effect of this scheme was immediate and dramatic. Within months, four new non-family partnerships were organized, each buying a good second-hand boat. All the new shareholders (over 20 of them) were young men who had previously been hired men on family boats, waiting their turn in a long queue for shares. It was now not only possible to jump the queue, but the queue itself soon disappeared entirely. In short, anyone who wanted a share could now have one by filling in a few forms.

The repercussions of this were felt by the family partnerships. Their hitherto secure control over labour began to crumble. They could no longer compete for the most ambitious and highly skilled young men, upon whom fishing success so greatly depends. Why, indeed, should an ambitious man settle for a job as a hired hand when he could make more money as his own boss? The owners of the family boats responded by giving regular bonuses and installing labour-saving machinery in an effort to make the jobs they were offering more attractive. They were still unable to get the men they would have liked, so they soon had to settle for anyone they could get, skilled or not, from Burra or else-where, including the Lerwick Labour Exchange — something unthinkable in the 1960s. Simultaneously, new oil-related jobs mopped up nearly all the surplus labour in Shetland. The only further response left open to the family partnerships was to reduce the size of their crews from eight men to seven, and then from seven to six, having only one hired man. This is where it now stands. With each concession they made, their profitability relative to non-family boats declined.

In 1978, the situation had been reached where, in one case in which there were two vacant shares in a family boat, in the absence of any other takers and desperate to stay in business, the three partners paid for the shares for two 17-year-old school leavers, the money being advanced to them until they qualified for the Highlands Board scheme on their eighteenth birthdays. Some partnerships have been even less successful. Four of the weakest family partnerships have gone broke since 1970, despite unprecedented fish prices. A few of their former shareholders now work as hired men on other Burra fishing boats or have taken shore jobs. No new family crews have been organized since the Highlands Board scheme came into operation.

In contrast, non-family partnerships have steadily increased in number; given another couple of years they will easily outnumber the remaining family partnerships. The non-family partnerships, too, have had their troubles getting enough hired men: there are now too many boats for the available labour in Burra, and because of oil, few men can be got from outside the island. Nevertheless, the non-family partnerships have managed to maintain crews of seven (as opposed to six), and compete among themselves for the best of the hired men who are available.

Another aspect of the effects of the Highlands Board scheme concerns economic and social status and control. The control of fathers and uncles over sons and nephews, in the past strengthened by their patrimonial favours, had greatly diminished. Younger men, in general, are no longer in a wholly dependent relation to their elders for their livelihood. The control over the means of production within the community has shifted from age to youth, from having the power to bestow patrimonies to the power to convert one's youthful energy directly into capital investment on one's own behalf, rather than someone else's. And, in consequence, one's status as a member of a kinship group now matters less than individual achievement.

Thus the Highlands Board scheme triggered off a chain of events that tipped the balance of factors of production from capital to labour, and the balance of factors of status (if one can coin such a phrase) from effective ascription by kin group to individual achievement. Superficially, at least, this is a return to the situation that obtained in the 1930s. Yet should the Highlands Board scheme come to an end at some future date, creating a scarcity of down payment money, it is not too difficult to visualize a return to the family partnership and patrimonial system.

Whether Burra has gained or lost as a result of the Highlands Board scheme is an arguable point. Certainly, there is a fairer and more even distribution of capital, and access to capital. Against this is the decline of kinship as an integrative institution (which I suspect anthropologists will tend to regret), and the loss of a neat, self-contained system of social control that has not, as yet, been replaced by anything equally effective. As fellow fishermen have no strong social obligations of the kind engendered by kinship and the expectation of patrimonies, crews are now much less stable over time than formerly. Disputes and broken partnerships are relatively common, where before they were rare. There are no clear rules, as there used to be, for organizing a partnership or recruiting new members into an existing one. Mistakes and confusion result. Given time, some more definite policies may develop: the Faroese, for example, are said to use political party membership as criterion of crew selection.

How does the concept of centre–periphery relations help us to answer the problem posed at the beginning of this paper: does it help the anthropologist to identify external factors and influences, to evaluate their status as evidence, and to accommodate them in his account of social reality? On the first of these three points, the notion of centre and periphery does indeed appear to help one identify the external causes and pressures for change, pointing up the ways in which the periphery is dependent upon the centre for certain things, and the dimensions and implications of its clientage. For example, we have seen that an increase in the level of transfer payments increases the dependency of the periphery upon the centre. For Burra fishermen, this dependency is now complete — 100% of the stake in fishing now comes from the centre, compared with zero before 1945. This has had a direct effect in reducing the importance of extended families as savings and loan associations. Independent, do-it-yourself financing on the local level is no longer necessary nor, apparently, desirable. State money may be dearer, because interest has to be paid, but family money has social costs. Evidently the social costs are thought to be more onerous than financial costs, judging from the choices that fishermen are presently making.

It also seems the case that increasing levels of transfer payments lead to a process of increased individuation, eroding the mutuality of interest in maintaining cooperative associations. In the past, a fisherman had a claim upon a family patrimony only by virtue of his relation to the capital holding group and his incorporation into it. As an outsider, unattached to a patrimonial group, he had no claims upon fishing capital.

Up to 1970, it could be seen that as boats became more expensive, the level of transfer payments increased because the payments were a fixed (85%) percentage of their cost. But it still left a critical margin of cost that kept the patrimonial system in business. After 1970, however, there was a change in the system of payment. The down payment limitation has now disappeared, and with it the rationale of the patrimonial group. This means, in effect, that isolated individuals now apply for their money directly to anonymous functionaries in a state institution. Kin group membership, to ensure one's claim on a patrimony, has become meaninglessly redundant. The relationship between the individual and the centre is now direct, no longer mediated by local social groupings.

The case of the fishermen is not unique in this respect. One could trace a similar process of individuation and the simultaneous decline of mutualities of social and economic interest in local or peripheral groupings with the introduction and proliferation of state social assistance schemes. Old age and disability pensions, maternity allowances, unemployment and supplementary benefits, for example, involve a direct relation between the individual recipient and the state ministry. Formerly, social insurance of a comparable sort was furnished by the extended family, by local patrons and benefactors or collectively by the local community. In Britain this last kind of assistance was usually called "parish relief". Relief was granted locally by the consent of one's neighbours in a district council meeting, and not by a distant and impersonal agency. One's claim to parish relief, therefore, was dependent upon one's membership and standing within a local community.

*A propos* the second point in our problem: does the notion of centre and periphery help us to evaluate the status, as evidence, of the external influences that impinge upon local communities? Here it would appear that the centre--periphery idea raises many more questions than it provides answers. What, in fact, are the sources of our information about the actions or intentions of the centre? Where does our evidence come from? How reliable is it? How do we regard, say, ministerial decisions or administrative directives? In what form do such things filter down to local level affairs? What are the grapevines of communication? As John Davis has pointed out, if we cannot do fieldwork in the councils and committees of higher levels of centrality, we are then forced to rely upon unverifiable gossip, rumour and speculation, leading us to conclusions of a kind that hold truth to be irrelevant (Davis, 1975:49). Of course, we can say that the actors' knowledge is all that matters, because that is what informs their behaviour. But if our ultimate purpose is to account for the changing relation between local communities and state institutions, for example, then we are unable to answer to this satisfactorily if we effectively ignore half the equation.

And what, exactly, is the other half of the equation? What is a "centre": in what does it reside or consist? Of pure analytical abstraction (Shils, 1975:1 ff.)? Of diffuse processes (Eisenstadt, 1973:30 ff.)?

Of places (Carter, 1974:307n)? Of bureaucracy, law, power or people? The proponents of the centre--periphery approach are remarkably unhelpful in providing hard operational criteria, frequently treating the concept of the "centre" as irreducible. If the centre does indeed consist of people making decisions in councils and committees, then at least theoretically this is a field that an anthropologist is well equipped to exploit. He need only identify who is central, in what way, and choose his informants accordingly. But in practice this may be an unrealistic goal. One would end up writing a short history of the world from the village street to the halls of Westminster and Brussels and the boardrooms of New York (*vide* Frank, 1978 and Wallerstein, 1974).

On the final part of the problem, how can "macro" and "micro" levels of analysis be accommodated in the same explanatory framework? Does bringing in the "macro" level of centre and periphery clarify or merely mystify? Is our account of why people behave as they do in particular situations made to explain anything more about their thoughts and actions by adding to it the dimension of depersonalized processes (Davis, 1975:49) in generalized situations? This of course is open to debate. Yet it would appear that the question of what constitutes evidence of the actions and intentions of the centre raises serious procedural difficulties about the way it enters our discussion of social reality (reality to whom?), and therefore how it can be handled within the same explanatory framework.

Said another way, what is the nature of the relation between centre and periphery? An adequate answer to this could be given by a description of the relations of power, dependency and clientage that obtain between them. The same answer would seem to serve whether this was posed as a "how" or a "why" question. "How are local communities peripheral to the centre?" and "Why are local communities peripheral to the centre?" in both cases can be answered perfectly well by describing the differentials in power, etc. between them.

Similarly, when we consider the nature of the response of local communities to the actions or intentions of the centre, it would appear that the question "How do local communities respond?" can be answered by classifying (describing) their possible responses. But, in contrast, if "why" is substituted for "how", the question demands quite a different sort of answer. A description of possible responses will not tell us why people in one place choose to respond in one way and not another. To say why, the answer must be sought internally, in the structure of social relations in particular communities, and not externally, in the generalities of power and dependency (cf. Brown, 1963). The notion of centre-periphery relations, it therefore appears to me, can help us only up to a point — to the point where explanation is called for. If, following Edmund Leach's dictum, it is the business of the anthropologist to attempt to explain social dealings, and not simply to classify or describe them, then there are limits to the contribution that externalist, macro-level paradigms can make to anthropological understanding (Leach, 1961).

Substantively, as well, I wonder just how much an analysis in terms of centre–periphery relations tells us that we did not already know or suspect, namely three things: (1) that within and between organizational levels it is possible to isolate relations of dominace and dependency; (2) that on virtually all levels beyond the local community itself, people in places like Burra are far more likely to be multiply peripheral than multiply central; and (3) that as central bureaucracies grow, competing associations, sodalities and mutualities on the periphery weaken as their powers are arrogated by the centre.

It seems to me that all of this was pointed out many years ago by Tönnies in his distinction between *Gemeinschaft* and *Gesellschaft* and by Max Weber in his remarks on the growth of bureaucracy. I am rather doubtful that despite its initial promise of permitting us to make the connections between local communities and wider processes and to analyse the macro- and micro-levels simultaneously, the centre-periphery model adds substantially to the understanding of case material such as I have described above, or to the understanding of what appears to be the essence of our problem in its European setting, bureaucratization. Certainly, the centre–periphery model covers the same ground, but I wonder if it is worth the effort simply to restate in different terms that which we already know.

## Acknowledgement

My field research in Shetland during 1971-73 was supported by a research fellowship from the Institute of Social and Economic Research, Memorial University of Newfoundland. During 1978-80 further fieldwork has been made possible by a grant from the North Sea Oil Panel, Social Science Research Council.

## References

Boissevain, J. and Friedl, J. (1975). "Beyond the Community: Social Process in Europe", Department of Educational Science of the Netherlands, The Hague.

Brown, R. (1963). "Explanation in Social Science", Routledge and Kegan Paul, London.

Carter, I. (1974). The highlands of Scotland as an underdeveloped region. *In* "Sociology and Development", (Eds E. DeKadt and G. Williams), Tavistock Publications, London.

Davis, J. (1975). Beyond the hyphen: Some notes and documents on community-state relations in south Italy. *In* "Beyond the Community: Social Process in Europe", (Eds J. Boissevain and J. Friedl), Dept. of Educational Science of the Netherlands, The Hague.

Eisenstadt, S. (1973). Traditional patrimonialism and modern neopatrimonialism. *Sage Research Papers in the Social Sciences* 1, 1-95. Sage Publications, London.

Frank, A. (1978). "World Accumulation 1492-1789", Macmillan Press, London.

Geertz, H. and Mills, C. (Eds) (1948). "From Max Weber: Essays in Sociology", Routledge and Kegan Paul, London.

Leach, E. (1961). "Rethinking Anthropology", Athlone Press, London.

Lofgren, O. (1972). Resource management and family firms: Swedish west coast fishermen. *In* "North Atlantic Fishermen", (Eds R. Andersen and C. Wadel), Memorial University of Newfoundland, St. John's.

Shils, E. (1975). "Centre and Periphery: Essays in Macrosociology", University of Chicago Press, Chicago.

Tönnies, F. (1955). "Community and Association", Routledge and Kegan Paul, London.

Wadel, C. (1974). Capitalisation and ownership: The persistence of fishermen-ownership in the Norwegian herring fishery. *In* "North Atlantic Fishermen" (Eds R. Andersen and C. Wadel), Memorial University of Newfoundland, St. John's.

Wallerstein, I. (1974). "The Modern World-system", Academic Press, London and New York.

# 10

# The Italian State and the
# Underdevelopment of South Italy

ROBERT WADE

In the 1970s "dependency theory" or "core–periphery analysis" has become, especially amongst younger scholars, the prevailing approach to the study of "underdeveloped" areas.[1] It is certainly more macroscopic than the dominant approach of the 1950s and 1960s, which saw the causes of development and underdevelopment, of "modernization" or "persistence of traditional society", as located primarily *within* national boundaries. The new approach, for all the diversity amongst its practitioners, looks for causes primarily in the *relations* between the institutions of the rich, industrialized parts of the globe, and those of the poorer parts. The external relationships of underdeveloped regions are held to dominate their internal dynamics: underdevelopment persists because the types of relations which exist between (dominant) core areas and (dependent, capitalist) peripheral areas cause in the latter "an aggravation of the structural characteristics of underdevelopment *pari passu* with growth" (Amin, 1974). The shift in emphasis from internal to relational aspects parallels similar shifts in other areas of the social sciences, reflecting a more explicit concern with the

151

analysis of power and subordination. So in the analysis of poverty in the United States, for example, one sees a similar change from the prevailing interpretation of the 1960s, that poverty persists because it is the way of life wanted by the poor, to the assumption of the 1970s, that poverty persists because those who are not poor want to maintain a social structure that includes a good many poor people (Gans 1972; Wade 1973).

The general danger of this approach is that analysis of these relations may substitute for analysis of the unit itself, whatever that unit may be. There is a tendency amongst dependency theorists to examine only those aspects of the dependent region which can be closely linked to the relationship with the core region, to take the analysis of the dependent region only to the point of illustrating the tendencies of the general dependency approach. One thereby loses a sense of the *local* interconnectedness of things — of the existence of connections between institutions shaped by the relations with dominant centres *and* other institutions whose form and meaning are little influenced by these relations (Schneider and Schneider, 1976; Amin, 1976). Insofar as particular cases are studied only as illustrations of general tendencies, there is a constant risk of tautology.

This paper suggests how core–periphery analysis can nevertheless provide a useful starting point for understanding South Italy's peculiar pattern of economic growth and social change, and how its too narrow view of social processes can be broadened to make it more satisfactory — and more relevant to anthropologists.

First a highly simplified core–periphery model of the world economy is sketched in barest outline. It is derived particularly from the work of Amin (1974, 1976) and Wallerstein (1974, 1977), but highlights ideas common to most "dependency" scholars.

## Core–Periphery Relations

We start by zoning the world economy into two territorial parts: a core, characterized by a high concentration of production *processes* (not final products) which are relatively highly mechanized, skill-intensive, and high-wage; and a periphery, characterized by a high concentration of labour-intensive, unskilled, low-wage processes. Hence one can speak of core states and peripheral states, depending on the concentration within their boundaries of core and peripheral production processes. But "core" and "periphery" are not to be defined merely in terms of such characteristics; the definition is inherently relational since "core" and "periphery" presuppose each other.

In *core economies*, a large part of production is for the domestic market. Where production is mostly organized for the pursuit of profit and the means of production are mostly privately owned, the owners and managers of each firm have an incentive to depress wages so as to increase the proportion of the firm's revenue left for profit. But declining wages throughout the economy would cause contraction of the domestic market: profits would fall as unsold stocks accumulated. Hence it is in the *collective* interest of the owners and managers of capital to have sustained market expansion, which is achieved by (1) increasing wages, and/or (2) increasing the dependence of rural households (especially formerly subsistence households) on the market. In this sense the interests of workers and capitalists are complementary, which provides a material basis for a sense of "nation" (Amin 1974: 599–600).

In *peripheral capitalist economies* a large part of production (excluding subsistence production) is for export, or for luxury consumption by a small, wealthy stratum. The interest of the owners and managers of capital (much of it from the core) is to keep wages low, so that the products may be competitive in international (core) markets, and/or low cost to the small, wealthy consuming stratum. The fact that a low average wage restricts the size of the domestic market is not important, for labour is only a cost to capital, not simultaneously a source of demand for products. In this situation the sense of *national* identity is for the great majority of the population (whatever the rhetoric of the political elite in control of the state) likely to be weak.

A large "subsistence" sector in the peripheral economy helps by (1) providing an abundant supply of cheap labour, (2) bearing part of the costs of reproduction of the labour force, since those engaged in the export or "modern" sectors normally get par of their support (not only while so engaged but more importantly in childhood, sickness and old age) from the subsistence sector, and do not have to rely wholly on wages to meet these costs; their wages can be correspondingly lower, and profits to the owners and managers of capital correspondingly higher.

So also does a large urban "informal" sector help to keep down the cost of labour to the modern or export sectors. Much of the consumption of modern or export sector employees is of products or services from the informal sector. Informal sector enterprises tend to be labour intensive, family based, and to offer low wages and poor (sub-legal) working conditions. Their products are thus relatively low cost, and the more of their products modern or export sector workers consume, the less those workers need be paid (since the consumption "yield" from a given wage level is multiplied by "informal" sector sources of supply); and therefore the more competitive their products in core country markets or in substituting for imports from core countries. This then is the primary role of the subsistence and informal sectors in global capital accumulation (Wallerstein, 1977; Amin, 1976, 1977; Portes, 1978).

The government of a peripheral state is likely to be in the hands of groups responsive to the requirements of the owners and managers of capital in the export and modern sectors, and thus to favour the preservation of "dependency" links with the core economies. It is likely to be repressive in the face of labour unrest, to keep down the cost of labour and preserve a "good climate" for foreign investors. (In any case, workers are less likely to be able to organize effectively than workers in the core.) The government is unlikely to give "informal" sector enterprises any advantage *vis-à-vis* modern sector enterprises in access to productive resources, or to enhance the productivity of "subsistence" sector households (which consume a high proportion of their output rather than deliver a surplus to the cities). That also would be against the interests of national capital accumulation, as shaped by the opportunities available in the relationship with the core.

Core enterprises will set up factories if strongly "site-attracted" (for example, to raw materials, or deep-water ports); or if "foot-loose" in search of cheap, unprotesting labourers, or minimal pollution controls; or if attempting to duck under tariff barriers to serve the elite-orientated domestic market. But the "disarticulated" nature of the peripheral economy means that the propulsive effect of these factories on the national economy is likely to be small; they are likely to remain outposts of the core economy. Moreover, migration of workers from the periphery to the core may avoid the need for cheap-labour-seeking core capital to move to them, preempting even the pretence of local development.

Economic growth in the peripheral capitalist economies is thus a reflex of the requirements of expansion in the core economies — for cheap inputs (raw materials, intermediate goods, labour), opportunities for investment, and market outlets. The pattern of growth is unlikely to meet the needs and aspirations of the mass of the population. It persists because it is *functional* for the interests of the dominant holders of power in both the core and in the periphery, though this is not to say that what happens is fully *intended* by representatives of either, especially the latter group. As long as things are working out as one wants — or not working out as one does not want — one does not have to intend to do things; they can be allowed to simply happen, and no action to change the outcome need be taken. But the consequences of the pattern of growth form essential elements of the cause, because wanted by the holders of power (Gans, 1972).

The model is manifestly crude, but not therefore necessarily absurd. It shows, above all, how one can look at world society as a whole, "from the outside", rather than beginning with the nation state and seeing the whole as an aggregate of more or less autonomous national systems. One can use it as a helpful "optic" without accepting the full-blown theoretical apparatus of Amin or Wallerstein.[2] The organizing concepts it presents can be elaborated and improved in various ways. It suggests first round explanations for major global trends in food production, industrialization, poverty, income distribution and forms of political conflict. In the second round different types of peripheries have to be distinguished (for example, those where core industrialists or traders are interested primarily in raw materials, or in export of cheap labour goods, or in the internal domestic market; those which have a large domestic marekt and are far from a core, those which are small and geographically close to a core (Seers, 1979; Bagchi, 1972). The model can be made less ahistorical (in practice the emphasis has fallen on distinguishing different stages of expansion of core economies, treating the history of peripheral areas as a reflex, but this is not a necessary consequences of the approach). And crude though it is, the model has some key propositions which can be confronted with evidence: for example the existence of a subsistence rural sector and/or a large informal urban sector is held to permit modern sector wages to be *lower* than they would otherwise be; are there by contrast circumstances when wages are *higher* than they would otherwise be because these sectors in fact provide alternative sources of income? But for anthropologists the area most in need of attention is likely to be the model's reduction of the social and political structure of the periphery to a mere epiphenomenon of the needs of capital accumulation. Amin treats variations in social and political structure from one part of the periphery to another as "appearances" masking the underlying essential similarity due to the *relation* of periphery to the core, as expressed primarily (as we have seen) in economic terms. Indeed, the sociology and politics of core-periphery relations have been much less intensively studied than the economics (but see Villamil (Ed.) 1979; Hopkins and Wallerstein, 1977). It is the interplay between "economic" and "non-economic" aspects we now examine in the specific context of South Italy.

## South Italian "Development"

The model of core-periphery relations described above deals essentially not with relations between states but between regions with high and low concentrations of certain kinds of production processes — whether within or across the boundaries of the entities called states. (The state apparatus is seen to be controlled by the owners and managers of big capital, and to have little independent significance.) So the fact that South Italy does not constitute a state does not rule out application of the model. South Italy has in fact a larger population than nearby peripheral Portugal and Greece combined (19 million), and it lies between them in terms of area. It includes 40% of Italy's area and 34% of the total population (1976).[3]

For centuries the region has played the role of a periphery in the European economy generally, and in particular of North Italy.[4] In 1951 average *per capita* income was just over half the average of the rest of the country;[5] unemployment and underemployment were endemic; over half the work force depended on an extensive, under-capitalized agriculture, as small owners, tenants, and labourers, frequently the same person being all three at once; the small manu-facturing sector was composed mainly of artisan "subsistence" units (with an average of fewer than three persons in each); investment was low, fertility high, and mass emigration had at times during the previous century reached torrential proportions. For centuries it exported agricultural products (cereals, sheep and cattle products, wine, olive oil) to core regions and imported manufactures and services — an exchange of low valued-added products in return for high valued-added products. There has always been relatively little trade *within* the South.

The self-conscious attempt to develop the South began in 1950, and has been sustained ever since. In terms of the investment resources made available (the investment rate has exceeded 25% of regional income ever since 1951, most of the resources coming from North Italy), the length of application, the statistical base, and the brilliance of the planners, the development programme for the South is rare amongst both developed and underdeveloped countries.

By the 1970s it was clear that a massive transformation of the South was well under way:

1. The proportion of the labour force in agriculture declined from 57% in 1951 to 27% by 1974 — the number of workers fell by over two million in 24 years.

Employment in "modern" industry (metallurgy, engineering, chemicals, petrochemicals, textiles) increased by 150 000 between 1961 and 1973; and since the plant for these industries is large-scale, there has also come the beginnings of a full-time industrial proletariat.

2. The South now has the bulk of Italy's new heavy industrial capacity.
3. Illiteracy declined from 24% of the population over five years old in 1951 to 11% in 1971.
4. Income per head grew by two and a half times between 1951 and 1971 (in real terms). Outside limited parts of Naples and Palermo one sees little evidence of severe poverty nowadays,[6] and The quality of *miseria*, an attitude of resigned fatalism which pervaded southern life, is now much attenuated. Those who have known the South over the past 25 years speak of a new sense of vigour and enterprise. An American anthropologist (Leonard Moss, personal communication) relates the following conversations with the same man, a southern peasant farmer:

> 1955 — "What of the future, Zi' Giovanni?"
> "For me the future is death, the cemetery."

> 1961 — (Same question.) "There is no future for me. But did I tell you, my daughter has been admitted to the *magistrale* (teacher training college)? She is the first of the family (to go on to higher education). And my son (grasping his son by the shoulder), he will go on to the university or I will break every bone in his body."

> 1968 — (Same question.) "I was watching television last night. The weather report says it will be warm and dry. The hazelnut will mature quickly and I shall get top price in the market."

On the negative side, however:

5. There has been massive emigration (over four million people quit the South from the early 1950s to the mid-1970s), despite which,
6: income per person remains at little more than *half* that in the North, as in 1951.
7. Unemployment remains high; 60% of Italy's registered unemployed live in the South (with 34% of Italy's population). Total employment *declined* by half a million between 1951 and 1975, at the same time as resident population has *increased* by almost one and a half million (the decline in employment is the result

mainly of rural exodus, unmatched — unlike the North — by a corresponding increase in urban employment). The irony is extreme: South Italy, plagued by problems of unemployment and underemployment, has a more capital-intensive, labour-saving set of new heavy industries than the North, alongside "subsistence" artisans and builders.

8.  Manufacturing activity in the South accounts for only 15% of value-added in manufacturing in Italy as a whole; agriculture remains by far the largest sector in terms of employment and value-added, although in terms of exports, the products of heavy industry (petrochemicals and metals) now equal agricultural products in value (Cafiero, 1976).

9.  The South's imports of goods and services have exceeded exports by a very large margin since the 1950s (at least). *Net* imports have amounted to 10-20% of total available resources since 1951; and have *increased* proportionately over time.

10. The trade deficit (much larger than any independent state could sustain) has been financed mainly by transfer payments, in the form of production subsidies, pensions, family allowances. These are transfers from northerners to southerners (indirectly via the state): there is a close positive correlation between the South's net imports and the volume of transfer payments paid to southerners, and a close inverse correlation for the North-west (around Milan, Turin, and Genoa) (Graziani, 1978; Graziani and Pugliese (Eds) 1979).

Social security payments are the major component of transfers. Such payments account for no less than 42% of total public expenditure (including investment) in Italy, and 11% of GDP. For their administration there are, it is estimated, 41 500 agencies (excluding wholly private or ecclesiastically controlled institutions) (Rogers and Moss, 1979)! Of the total payments, about 70% is accounted for by pensions alone (old age, disablement, widowhood). The monetary value of social security payments has grown between 1971 and 1975 at five times the growth of GDP.

While transfer payments are clearly a vital element in the working of the Italian economy at large, they weigh even more heavily in the South than in the North. The South receives almost *twice* as much in social security payments as its people contribute. The number of pensions going to the South increased by 29% in the five between 1971 and 1975, double the rate of increase in the North. Most of the increase in pensions in the South has been of the "disabled person" type (a point I return to).

## *Needs of Northern Capitalists*

How can this curious pattern of "development" be explained? Most of the development literature on "the southern problem" (and it is large) stresses "internal" reasons why the South has not had a more balanced, employment-creating development. South and North are assumed to be more or less distinct economies, with no important causal connection between the North's progress and the South's under-development. Indeed, the further progress of the North is seen as a necessary condition for more underdevelopment in the South, to provide still more resources for overcoming the South's various "internal" obstacles and reducing its population by migration (Lutz, 1962; Schachter, 1965; Italy, Ministero del Bilancio, 1972; OECD, 1976; Banfield, 1958). Anthropological interpretations of the South, insofar as they address such issues at all, tend to be consistent with the "internal" explanation.

The core–periphery model suggests a different view. The failure to reach the announced development objectives (such as equalization of *per capita* income between North and South) can be seen not as the result of accident or inefficiency or corruption or "Mafia" (the kind of explanation which strictly local-level studies might suggest) but the result of a divergence between stated objectives and "real" objectives. The "real" objectives are derived from the requirements of the owners and managers of large-scale, *northern*-based Italian capital; and the actual results of the southern development programme described earlier have been *functional* for these requirements (see Garofoli, 1976).

The first requirement was for a supply of cheap labour available as needed for *northern* industry. The second was for a new, modern heavy industry sector, to supply basic inputs to intermediate and consumer goods industries. The third (which emerged later in time) was for an expanding domestic market for northern manufacturers.

Simplified, the argument is as follows. Following post-war recon-struction the Italian government had two basic choices: to opt immediately for a set of economic policies to bring about high employment throughout the country (including the South); or to go for export-led growth, relying on the growing market for manufactured products in Western Europe. It chose the latter, because of the pre-existing dominance of northern industrialists in the political alliance which ruled the country. Export-led growth produced the very high rates of growth of GNP in the late 1950s and early 1960s, the "economic boom". But its motor was low wages, for only with low wages could

Italian products be competitive. For this purpose, a reserve of labour in the South was functional. In the first phase of state intervention in the South, the land reform created a mass of small farms, too small for reinvestment and productivity growth. In this situation the farmers were ready to move off the land and sell their labour whenever opportunities for slightly higher incomes arose. In the second phase, after the early 1960s, the insertion of large, capital-intensive plants created few new jobs in relation to the size of the investment (between 1951 and 1971 industrial investment increased 700%, and industrial employment increased 45%), and probably worsened the competitiveness of the artisan sector by attracting skilled workers from it. With these types of intervention the labour supply ready to move from the South to northern industry remained ample, thus ensuring the maintenance of low wage levels in northern industry. A more employment-orientated use of the investment resources in the South would have impaired this process.

The cheap labour policy was one means to high profits for northern industrialists. The second was a large new basic industrial sector to supply them with relatively cheap and securely available inputs. This, however, required enormous investment resources, higher than those available to private industrialists. The price they were prepared to pay was a growing public sector control over basic industries, in return for *state* (rather than private) financing. It mattered that the new state-controlled industries were complementary to, not competitive with, the products of northern private industry, and thus the extension of state ownership looked less threatening than otherwise. But why were the new industries located in the South? Because of lower land prices (the new heavy industries required much land), easier access to sea transport (important since their raw materials — especially oil and ores — come by sea), less opposition to industrial pollution, and an unsaturated infrastructure (especially housing for workers). Moreover, the "multiplier effects" of the expenditure generated by the southern plants — the expenditure on equipment, for example — would, in the absence of a broadly based industrial sector in the South, come back to the North; again the "costs" of a southern location would be lessened. The prediction was correct; the big plants have remained "cathedrals in the desert", having little stimulating effect on local enterprise, and with control of production remaining firmly in the North (Amin predicts this pattern to be a characteristic tendency in the whole of the (global) periphery — Amin, 1976:201). Finally, the state announced a large and elaborate incentive scheme to give financial inducements for industrialists (including managers of *state*-holding companies) to locate in the South; but made the size of the inducement dependent on the amount of *capital* employed, not labour. (By the late 1960s the financial incentives were the highest on offer within the EEC.) So, under cover of a great *national* objective — the development of the South — a means was provided for subsidizing the costs of inputs to northern private industrialists.

The industrial intervention strategy thus fitted well the requirements of northern industrialists.

In the 1960s, as Italian wage levels rose in relation to those of competitors, northern manufacturers became more interested in the domestic market as an outlet for their products. The South presented obvious opportunities. Transport difficulties prior to the early 1960s helped to protect a small-scale manufacturing sector producing for local markets within the South. Since then, the opening up of the South by means of vastly improved road, rail and air networks (as part of the development plan) had the effect of making the South an open economy. Northern manufacturers in search of economies of scale found that the cost of exporting to the South had fallen. A commercial invasion from the North became worthwhile. Between 1961 and 1973 the traditional manufacturing sectors in the South (food, clothing, leather, furniture, etc.) lost some 60 000 jobs, while in the North employment in the *same* sectors *increased* by 40 000. Local producers were backwashed out of existence. However, without increases in southern monetary incomes the opportunities for sales would have been very limited. It is in overcoming this problem that the huge volume of transfer payments into the South has been important, as a way of monetizing southern incomes (even if still at a low level) so as to make southerners effective market consumers — of *northern* products. For example, a study of consumer goods retailers in Campania (excluding Naples, the capital) showed that in 1975 over half their sales of clothing, household furnishings, fresh and preserved meat, drinks, milk and cheese, were of products from outside the South (Narni-Mancinelli, n.d.). Thus, through the transfer payments type of intervention, the growth of some parts of northern industry could be supported.

This interpretation of the South's development pattern sees what took place in the South as a "reflexive", dependent type of develop-ment, reflecting the interests of the owners and managers of Italian big capital, in the North. The South had a vital role in these interests — but not one conducive to its broad-based development. The inter-pretation is thus a variant of the general core–periphery model described earlier; the South's experience is understood as shaped by the "needs of capital accumulation" in the core.[7]

While this is a better starting point for understanding the South's development than assuming the South to be a more or less distinct entity from the North (and in some versions giving *primary* causal weight to southern social structure and values), it is obviously much too simply; at this point, the mind cannot come to rest. For one thing, the natural environment of the South *is* much less conducive to economic progress than the North's; the South *is* farther from the core markets of Europe than the North; and class relations in the southern countryside have been less conducive to rises in labour productivity than in the North (Silverman, 1968; Brenner, 1977). Most importantly for our purposes, the above interpretation of the South, like the general core--periphery model, assumes a much too passive role of the state as a simple instrument of the capitalist class.

## Need for the State's Legitimacy

The content and results of development policy for the South have been strongly shaped by the competition between political groupings for electoral support. The process of political competition is partly separate, in a causal sense, from the processes included in the core-periphery model, and in turn affects them in important ways.

The fact that the South is part of the same state as the North in some ways reduces its bargaining power (by removing the tariff instrument, for example). In another way its power is greatly enhanced, because the central government has to be supported by southern votes or risk electoral defeat. (In the 1950s and 1960s the vote for the Christian Democrat and right-wing parties coming from the South accounted for not much less than *half* their total vote in national elections.) This brings the "ruling" classes of the North — if ruling is the right word — to enter alliances with those classes of southern Italy which can guarantee election results. The latter *might* use their bargaining power to promote the transformation of the South in line with the needs, in some sense, of the mass of southerners, because they see this as a necessary condition for retaining political power.

The reality has been different. Before World War II the class which could guarantee elections and social order was the landlords, in control of the vital income-earning asset. They had little interest in raising productivity, having the (state-backed) power to increase their incomes by raising the rental share, reducing the size of plot and contractual security, or making their labourers work harder and longer. After World War II and the land reform the best allies for the dominant class of the North became the rapidly growing class of bureaucrats who administer public expenditure, controlling access to the state Treasury (the new vital income-earning asset). The bureaucrats have used their control over personal subsidies, the capital and labour markets to secure votes.

The number of state functionaries in the South has grown by 73% between 1951 and 1973 (against a national average of 70%). The South now has the same proportion of Italy's state functionaries as its population; but since unemployment is higher in the South the weight of public administration in total employment is substantially greater in the South. For every employee in public administration in the South (1973) there are 1.5 employees in manufacturing industry; in the North-west, 6.4. Moreover, while the average income of state functionaries in the South is about the same as in the North, the average income in other sectors is lower and more insecure; hence a job in public administration in the South is worth much more in relation to alternatives than one in the North. (In 1973 the average income in public administration in the South was twice that in industry; in the North, only fractionally higher.)

The power of the public administration in the South is constantly growing. With the decline of traditional industries, the abandonment of an unproductive agriculture, and the now limited prospects for emigration, livelihoods in the South are increasingly coming to depend on access to the state Treasury and employment in big plants. This access is controlled (or strongly influenced) by state functionaries. They have a triple control: on the capital market, because subsidies, special credit, all sorts of authorizations go through their hands; on the labour market, because they can influence the choice of who will be employed in the big plants and the public service; and on the distribution of social security payments. Because of the importance of personal relations in southern bureaucracy — resources are relatively free-floating and can be obtained if only the right personal connections are made — an important functionary in one sector (e.g. pensions) is able, to a greater degree than is normal in the North, to use his position to secure the personal contacts needed to exert influence in other sectors (e.g. employment in big plants). In this way people in public administration can influence all sectors of southern Italian life, and take a hand in an enormous range of economic initiatives. And conversely, there is a "psychological backwash" on attitudes towards industry, because much energy and investment which could be channelled into productive enterprise is channelled instead into trying to secure a state post (Ryan 1977, p. 76).

The typical political formation of the South contains a high level leader of a party faction in Rome, able to influence the spending of one or more government departments, backed up by followers at the regional or provincial level able to guarantee the high-level leader (or leaders) a safe seat. The followers may be state functionaries who owe their jobs to the faction leader, members of the regional or provincial party federations, or members of predatory organizations like the Mafia.

The political process is a constant struggle between factions for control of key areas and resources. Party organization is weak, and voting patterns unstable compared to the North as first one, then another faction comes to prominence in a given area.

The consequence of this process is that development projects and policies which escape the control of leading factions are liable to be sabotaged by them: better no development at all than development which escapes their control. This form of political organization thus generates pressures in the South for expansion of state posts, increases in subsidies, investment in big plant, discretionary protection to (often inefficient) small firms of the "traditional" sector (including family farms of the hills and mountains), and social security payments: all of these are readily tradeable for political support.

One understands from this perspective why most of the increase in state pensions in the South in the 1970s has been of the "disabled person" type: its allocation criteria are more flexible than for the other sorts of pensions, it is available to persons of younger age, and it is an advantage for getting many public sector jobs since it is taken as proof of disablement, and disabled persons have preferential access to certain public jobs. In short, it is especially important in clientele politics.

The arguments then is this: the failure of employment to increase in the South after the 1950s, which was only partly offset by heavy emigration, created a potentially dangerous threat to the social order. The government strategy consisted of obligations on the state holding companies to locate most of their new investment in the South, an expansion of the government bureaucracy, a concentration of resources in the hands of state functionaries, an expansion of aids to (capital-intensive) industry, grants to farmers, and personal subsidies of various kinds. In this way (1) the government could be seen to be doing something on a massive scale for the South, and (2) resources could be channelled to supporters of the ruling parties and various factions within them, via long chains of patrons, clients and brokers. One effect of these measures was to keep personal income and consumption increasing in line with the rest of the country. But since the South did not, and still does not, have the conditions for flexible supply in response to increased demand, much of the increase in incomes was spent on northern-made goods and services; which has destroyed more pre-existing productive capacity in the South. Hence the large balance of trade deficit with the North continues to grow. Hence the need for subsidies continues, despite the huge inflow of investment to produce goods for export to the North.

The transfers come via the state apparatus. The power of state functionaries thus continues to grow, as more of the southern population become dependent in one way or another on transfers. Hence the governing parties are able to continue to get electoral majorities, and remain in office.

It is not just southern politicians and state functionaries *in the South* who have these interests. Southerners, orientated to jobs in public administration and politics, have come to acquire a grossly disproportionate hand in the public administration and politics of the country at large (Allum, 1973), as holders of high office in the political parties, the parliament, the trade unions, the state holding companies, the police — all of which helps to explain the absence of "southern nationalism".[8] The "southernization" of the state, it has been called. They are able to use their position to influence decisions about *national* policy (not only that directed specifically at the South) so as to protect the people and the clientele structures on which they depend. At a time when their rule is under sustained attack, the Christian Democrat party and its allies are unlikely to abandon the support they get through these various clientelistic means — even if the peculiar pattern of "development" we have seen is the by-product.

## Synthesis

We now have two rather different answers to the question of why the huge flow of (state) investment into the South has done little to promote a vigorous industrialization, able to increase the demand for labour in the South and increase income levels fast enough to catch up with the rest of the country. The first is in terms of the "needs of capital", which sees such an industrialization as against the interests of the owners and managers of Italian big capital, who are located in the North, and who exert a preponderant influence on state policies. The second is in terms of the "need for legitimacy" of the ruling parties, their need to get electoral support and to *strengthen* the autonomy of the state. The first answer thus sees transfer payments, for example, as a means of promoting the growth of some parts of northern industry; the second, as a means of securing electoral majorities from the South for the ruling parties (and containable discontent).

The two answers are not, however, mutually exclusive. It is likely that the tendencies highlighted by both are both operating, and the observed outcome the result of a complex interplay (more like the strands of a double helix than a dialectical synthesis). The Italian state is not simply the instrument of capitalist class interests, unable to intervene powerfully against those interests; but nor is it so autonomous from that dominant class that it can sustain intervention to secure political support regardless of the effects on capital accumulation. On the one hand, the political structures limit the extent to which the tendencies derived from the "needs of capital" are realized on the ground. Whereas the simple "needs of capital" argument implies that the new industry located in the South functions as (or more) efficiently there than it would have in the North (it was put there because northern industrialists thought a southern location optimal in terms of national capital accumulation), the evidence seems to suggest (though it is yet too sparse to be conclusive, see Chapman 1977 and 1978), that this industry is relatively *inefficient*, because vulnerable to manipulation at the hands of rival political factions. Where firms compete mainly to get state subsidies and purchasing contracts the results are likely to be different from and more inefficient than market competition: plant which is too small and dispersed, in order to get funds to all the various factions in a coalition; agglomerates which are too big, in order to prevent state funds from flowing to rivals. It has become a favourite ploy, especially in chemicals, to plan a costly plant, pocket the financial assistance, then bankrupt the company. The steel-works at Goia Tauro is a glaring example of a huge subsidized investment undertaken largely to finance local political factions loyal to a particularly powerful Minister; but the location was known in advance to be quite inappropriate for such a project (a whole new port had to be constructed), and the project has now been heavily scaled-down, after many millions of lire have been spent through it. Significantly, *Confindustria*, the main body representing big (northern) companies has tended to be critical of state policies to induce firms to move South, both publicly and still more in private lobbying (Chapman, personal communication).

It appears, then, that South Italy is a case where the effects of state intervention in the name of "development" have often been *against* the interests of the owners and managers of (productive) capital — where the "needs of capital accumulation on a national scale" have been (partially) sacrificed as a by-product of the semi-autonomous struggle for political support.

On the other hand, the "needs of capital" set limits on the extent to which the state can operate against national capital accumulation in pursuit of clientelistic political support in the South. In a competitive world economy, the crisis in national capital accumulation, to which inefficient "modern" heavy industry in the South is a substantial contributor, is expressed in the country's chronic balance of payments deficit; which in turn prompts other adjustments, such as deflationary measures wanted by the country's creditors. These in turn prompt reactions from those who feel deprived or threatened, one of which may be a switch in political party support, producing a change in the basis of legitimacy, and perhaps a change in the balance of class forces.

The alliance of the new southern bureaucratic elite with the northern industrialists through the state is thus the partial equivalent at country level of Sunkel's transnationalization thesis (1973): elites of peripheral states integrate their interests with those of the owners and managers of transnational capital, using the state apparatus to redistribute part of the surplus to themselves. But in the South Italian case, in contrast to the normal assumption in core-periphery analysis, the effects of that redistribution of surplus have been *harmful* in some ways to the interests of northern industrialists. The "logic of capital accumulation" is refracted by the political and social structure, and in the South Italian case partially undermined by it.

This interpretation of the role of the state in South Italy raises questions about the connection between state power and class power in capitalist states — which will not, however, be pursued here (Miliband, 1973; Parkin, 1979). Rather, the point here is that with the "refraction" perspective we can indeed, as Mills suggests (see quotation cited in Chapter 1 of this volume, p. 1), have our cake and eat it too: we can incorporate into the analysis the global tendencies, without denying the often decisive importance of purely national features and local circumstances. It is especially in studying how the refraction of the macroscopic trends by politics and social structure takes place on the ground — the social characteristics of the individuals and groups involved, the meanings they give its manifestations, how they cope with the constraints and opportunities it sets, the impact of the refraction on the structures themselves — that anthropologists can make an important contribution. In the final two decades of the twentieth century the global integration of production will come to impinge still more forcefully than in the recent past on the life of ordinary people in town, countryside and city. Anthropologists will have to comprehend and address themselves to that context. Who would study a seashore without knowing about the tides?

## Acknowledgement

This paper builds on two earlier papers on the South's "development" (Wade, 1977, 1979). My thanks go to Susan Joekes for comments on the first draft.

## Notes

[1] The literature is large, much of it not in English. In English, see Palma (1978), Sunkel (1979), Valenzuela and Valenzuela (1979), Foster-Carter (1976), Amin (1974, 1974a, 1976), and Hopkins and Wallerstein (1977). For case studies, see Leys (1975), Schneider and Schneider (1976). For a sceptical view see Brenner (1977).

[2] For instance, one need not agree with two of Amin's most stoutly argued propositions: that the analysis of differences between nation states in the periphery is necessarily superficial, because such differences mask the underlying similarities (see for example 1974; 166-167); and that "proper" development is only possible for a state by breaking out of the world capitalist system completely (see 1974;131). On Wallerstein, Brenner (1977) provides a powerful critique; yet his analysis leads us back towards seeing the globe as an assemblage of more or less autonomous state/class systems, and misses the critical distinction between two fundamental tendencies, (a) towards the integration of production on a world scale, and (b) towards the formation of, and struggle for control of, strong national states (Hopkins and Wallerstein, 1977:113).

[3] "The South" is normally taken to be the area of the former Kingdom of Two Sicilies. Its northern boundary is a line which starts just south of Rome and runs north-east across the peninsula.

[4] I make no attempt here to explore the deep historical roots of the South's underdevelopment and peripheral status *vis-à-vis* the North. As an introduction, see Procacci (1968).

[5] Much of the statistical data in the paper comes from Graziani and Pugliese (1979), Cafiero (1976), and various SVIMEZ and ISTAT publications (see references). Details on sources are given in Wade (1977, 1979).

[6] Montegrano, the town studied by Edward Banfield in the mid-1950s and analysed in his book, "The Moral Basis of a Backward Society" (1958)

(today still one of the most popular studies of southern society), now has a distinct air of prosperity. Yet Banfield argued that the prosperity of Montegrano (which he took to be typical of South Italy) depended heavily on the development of civic consciousness and the ability to sustain formal associations. Montegrano's prosperity has come without such a development (it still has very few of the civic associations or political parties whose active presence Banfield took to be a necessary condition for economic development). Of course, neither Banfield nor most other students of the South predicted the massive increase in transfer payments on which the South's present prosperity rests, which I analyse below.

(7) The North during the export-led growth phase was intermediate between the Western European core and its own southern periphery; it drew cheap labour from the South, and exported cheap-labour goods to Western European markets. This reminds us that in empirical applications, the simple core–periphery distinction is too simple. Hopkins and Wallerstein (1977) discuss the need for a third logical category in their analysis, that of semi-periphery.

(8) cf. Hirschman's critique of Myrdal's "backwash" thesis of growing regional polarisation: '. . . his preoccupation with the mechanism of cumulative causation hides from him the emergence of strong forces making for a turning point once the movement towards North–South polarisation within a country has proceeded for some time' (1958, p. 187).

## References

Allum, P. (1973). "Italy — Republic Without Government", Weidenfeld and Nicholson, London.

Amin, S. (1974). "Accumulation on a World Scale: A Critique of the Theory of Underdevelopment", Monthly Review Press, New York.

Amin, S. (1974a). "Accumulation and development: a theoretical model", *Rev. African Pol. Econ.* 1 (1), 9-26.

Amin, S. (1976). "Unequal Development: An Essay on the Social Formations of Peripheral Capitalism", Harvester Press, Sussex.

Amin, S. (1977). "Imperialism and Unequal Development", Harvester Press, Sussex.

Bagchi, A. (1972). "Some international foundations of capitalist growth and underdevelopment", *Econ. Pol. Weekly* Special Number, August, 1559-1570.

Banfield, E. (1958). "The Moral Basis of a Backward Society", The Free Press, New York.

Brenner, R. (1977). "The origins of capitalist development: a critique of neo-Smithian Marxism", *New Left Rev.* 104, 25-93.

Cafiero, S. (1976). "Svilluppo Industriale e Questione Urbana nel Mezzogiorno", SVIMEZ, Giuffre.

Chapman, G. (1977). "The political aspects of development in Southern Italy", unpublished manuscript, University of Sussex.

Chapman, G. (1978). "Theories of development and underdevelopment in southern Italy", *Dev. Change* **9**, 365-396.

Foster-Carter, A. (1976). "From Rostow to Gunder Frank: conflicting paradigms in the analysis of underdevelopment", *World Dev.* **4(3)**, 169-180.

Gans, H. (1972). "The positive functions of poverty", *Am. J. Sociol.* **78(2)**, 275-289.

Garofoli, G. (1976). "Un'analisi critica della politica di riequilibrio regionale in Italia: il caso del Mezzogiorno". *In* "Mezzogiorno e Crisi", (Ed. F. Indovina), Franco Angeli, Milano.

Graziani, A. (1978). "The Mezzogiorno in the Italian Economy", *Cam. J. Econ.* **2(4)**.

Graziani, A. and Pugliese, E. (Eds.) (1979). "Investimenti e Disoccupazione nel Mezzogiorno", Il Mulino, Bologna.

Hirschman, A. (1958). "The Strategy of Economic Development", Yale University Press, New Haven, CT.

Hopkins, T. and Wallerstein, I. (1977). "Patterns of development of the modern world-system", *Review I* **(2)**, 111-145.

Italy, ISTAT (1975). "Annuario di Contabilita Nazionale, 1974", Vol. II, Roma.

Italy, ISTAT (1976). "II° Censimento Generale delle Populazione, 24 Ott. (1971)", Vol. X, Roma.

Italy, ISTAT (1977). "Annuario di Statistiche del Lavoro", Roma.

Italy, Ministero del Bilancio (1972). "Programme Economico Nazionale, 1971-1975".

Leys, C. (1975). "Underdevelopment in Kenya, The Political Economy of Neo-Colonialism", Heinemann, London.

Lutz, V. (1962). "Italy, A Study in Economic Development", Oxford University Press, Oxford.

Miliband, R. (1973). "Poulantzas and the capitalist state", *New Left Rev.* **82**.

Narni-Mancinelli, E. n.d. (1977). "Produzione locale e concorrenza esterna nell'area delle grande industria". Manuscript at the Centro di Specializzazione e Richerche Economico-Agrarie per il Mezzogiorno, Portici, Naples.

OECD (1976) Italy, *In* "Regional Problems and Policies in OECD Countries", Vol. 1, Paris.

Parkin, F. (1979). "Marxism and Class Theory: A Bourgeois Critique", Tavistock, London.

Portes, A. (1978). "The informal sector and the world economy: notes on the structure of subsidised labour", *IDS Bulletin* **9(4)**:35-40, Institute of Development Studies, Sussex.

Procacci, G. (1968). *"History of the Italian People"*, Weidenfeld and Nicholson, London.

Rogers, E. and Moss, D. (forthcoming). Poverty in Italy, *In* "Poverty and Inequality in the Common Market Countries", (Ed. V. George and R. Lawson), Routledge Kegan Paul, London.

Ryan, D. (1977). The University of Calabria in its regional context, *Paedagogica Europaea* **VII** (1).

Schachter, G. (1965). "The Italian South", Random House, New York.

Schneider, J. and P. (1976). "Culture and Political Economy in Western Sicily", Academic Press, London, and New York.

Seers, D., Schaffer, B., Kiljunen, M.-L. (Eds) (1979). "Underdeveloped Europe: Studies in Core-Periperhy Relations", Harvester Press, Sussex.

Silverman, S. (1968). Agricultural organisation, social structure, and values in Italy: amoral familism reconsidered, *Am. Anthropol.* **70**, 1-18.

Sunkel, O. (1973). "Transnational capitalism and national disintegration in Latin America", *Soc. Econ. Studies* **22**, (1).

Sunkel, O. (1979). The development of development thinking, *In* "Transnational Capitalism and Development: New Perspectives on Dependence", (Ed. J. Villamil), Harvester Press, Sussex.

SVIMEZ (1977). "Il sistema pensionistico dell'INPS nel Mezzogiorno", *Informazioni SVIMEZ* **XXX**, No. 9.

Valenzuela, J. and Valenzuela A. (1979). Modernisation and dependence: Alternative perspectives in the study of Latin American underdevelopment, *In* "Transnational Capitalism and National Development: New Perspectives on Dependence", (Ed. J. Villamil), Harvester Press, Sussex.

Villamil, J. (Ed.) (1979). "Transnational Capitalism and National Development: New Perspectives on Dependence", Harvester Press, Sussex.

Wade, R. (1973). A culture of poverty?, *IDS Bulletin* **5** (2/3), Institute of Development Studies, Sussex.

Wade, R. (1977). Policies and politics of dualism: the Italian case, *Pacific Viewpoint* **18**(2), and *ids Discussion Paper* 106.

Wade, R. (1979). Fast growth and slow development in South Italy, *In* "Underdeveloped Europe: Studies in Core-Periphery Relations", (Eds D. Seers, B. Schaffer and M.-L. Kiljunen), Harvester Press, Sussex.

Wallerstein, I. (1974). "The Modern World System: Capitalist Agriculture and the Origins of the European World-Economy in the Sixteenth Century", Academic Press, London and New York.

Wallerstein, I. (1977). Rural economy in modern world-society. *Studies in Comparative International Development* **XII(I)**, 29-40.

# 11

## *Centre–Periphery as a Concept for the Study of the Social Transformation of Turkey*

*ŞERIF MARDIN*

In this volume, "Centre–Periphery" has been used primarily in the context of dependency theory, but there is another use of the concept which may be traced to Edward Shils' work. In Shils' use, "Centre" refers to a principle which enables society to function as a collectivity; it is a core feature which turns that society into more than a random collection of individuals and groups. The periphery, on the other hand, is that part of society which takes its sightings from the Centre (Shils, 1961).[1]

In Shils' use, both "centre" and "periphery" are abstractions: they refer to a polarity which underlies social organization. S. N. Eisenstadt, further underlining the institutional component of this polarity, has used "centre" to denote the concentration of ideological, organizational and technological instrumentalities in the central command mechanism of a polity. In Eisenstadt's use, among the functions of a "centre" figure those of a government and administration as well as the structuring of the cosmic and the "social and moral order" (Eisenstadt, 1973; Mardin, 1972).

Eisenstadt's reformulation of the centre–periphery concept enables us to underline a few salient characteristics of the political system of contemporary Turkey. These features appear first in the Ottoman state, and the extent of their transformation as well as the extent to which they still survive is what interests us here. Thus centre–periphery relations, as a framework for analysis, enables us to highlight what, at first sight appears improbable, namely the continuity between the basic "code" used by Ottoman statesmen in setting guidelines for statesmanship and the "code" used by the founders of the secular Turkish Republic for the same purpose. Secondly, centre–periphery relations enable us to shed some light on the nature of the tactical errors perpetrated both by these founding fathers and a large group of Turks influenced by their outlook after the introduction of multi-party politics in Turkey in the 1950s. This constant "lack of fit" between political maps of reality and the larger spectrum of political forces which we, in our hindsight, are able to observe, continues to plague many analysts of political events in Turkey today. This rubric would include political parties, intellectuals and members of the civilian and military bureaucracy but is not limited to them.

## History

The central mechanism of political and social control established by the Ottoman State constituted a successful solution to a problem which had plagued Middle East dynasties for centuries. (Gellner, 1970; Waterbury, 1970; Inalcik, 1973). These dynasties often crumbled after an initially successful bid to found a state because they could not harness the necessary resources that would build a machinery of political and social control. Dynasties were challenged by princelings or local notables or tribal leaders who could summon their own forces against those of the incipient state. The rulers, on the other hand, had difficulties building a bureaucracy and a military force which was entirely dependent on them.

A typical example of a military force not fully integrated with the centre was the employment by the state of tribal contingents. The allegiance of these contingents went first to their chief and only then to the ruler. The Ottomans experienced bitter disappointments with the insubordination or the defection of such troops at the time of the formation of the Empire. To remedy them was one of their major concerns.

Another example of "ascriptive" loyalties which had to be overcome by the state in order to establish an integrated central bureaucratic mechanism may be given from a much later stage in the history of the Ottoman Empire. Even after the formation of the Ottoman state some practices were instituted which were still reminiscent of a "patchwork" structure rather than of Weber's rational bureaucracy. Thus, in the eighteenth century, when the need for translators into Western languages increased due to the contacts of the Porte with the Western states, the translators for the Ottoman "Ministry of Foreign Affairs" were recruited from the ranks of a sub-ethnic group, i.e. from the elite of Greek subjects of the Empire known as Phanariot Greeks. Eventually, the services of these translators had to be dispensed with because it was found that their allegiance went first to their own ethnic--religious group (Mardin, 1962). During the nineteenth century, however, many Phanariot families continued to serve as links between the West and the Ottoman State.

The segmented structure of Ottoman society appeared once more in the economic organization of Ottoman lands. Here, the division of labour had a strong ethnic component. As late as 1917 this feature was described as follows:

> The occupational structure in Turkey coincides in many respects with racial differentiation. The social stratification which is thus determined can be traced in the manifold gradations of the national structure. Each single ethnic community is, as it were, a mesh in the greater economic web of the Empire and its removal would leave in the general economic life a gap which could not be readily filled up . . . (Issawi, 1966).

We may picture the Ottoman state, then, as made up of various ethnic, religious, regional and tribal groups brought together by a machinery of the state which was able to draw out of all of them the resources needed to keep the whole together. Even exemptions to various forms of taxation were meant to keep the forces of the centre from being squandered.

The Ottomans scored many successes in surmounting the structural impasses with which they started. They were able to attach to the political centre a corps of foot soldiers who, through a complicated system of recruitment and training, were cut off from their ascriptive ties. The same system applied to the training and recruitment of the military and bureaucratic personnel of higher rank. Other features came to reinforce this basic structure. A cast of scribes kept detailed fiscal records. A hierarchy of Doctors of Islamic Law filled judicial and educational posts. Provincial administration took the state into provincial centres. All of these institutions established a *relatively* dense network of bureaucratic transactions in the daily life of the Ottoman (Shaw, 1976:115 ff.). The ideological counterpart of this organizational sophistication was the concept of *Devlet* (the state). Usually used as *Din-u-Devlet* (the State and Religion). Of these two, the state had a relative position which was unknown up to that time in the Middle East, in particular, because the Ottomans developed a "law of the state" divergent in its outline from the *Seriat*, the basic religious law. *Devlet* thus meant more *raison d'Etat* than simply *Etat* and *"siyaset"* the equivalent of the concept of "the political" was also the word denoting a death sentence passed on an official (Mumcu, 1963). Because Ottoman officials were recruited by methods that cut them off from ascriptive ties they were, literally "state men", men with loyalty only to the state (Toynbee, 1951–61, V, 50; III, 34).

The successes of the Ottoman Empire were as much successes of classification as they were achievements in political and social resource concentration. The Empire dealt with the extraordinary variety of peoples over which it had established its rule by classifying them according to some principal religions practised in the Empire. The classification has usually been named the *millet* system, but the term itself derives from the later practice of the nineteenth century. This classification, however, concealed a number of difficulties which became apparent with time. The Ottomans, for instance, classified the Greeks, the Bulgarians, the Serbs and the Rumanians as belonging to the Orthodox *millet*. This did injury to the fact that the Bulgarians and the Serbs had at one time had autonomous churches with separate religious "capitals". During the nineteenth century with the rise of nationalism and the resurgence of these old entities it became extremely difficult to accommodate these sub-groups within the Orthodox *millet* under one single umbrella (Shaw, 1976:58-59, 134-135, 151-153).

The same conditions prevailed for the Muslim populations of the Ottoman Empire. Nominally, there was only one ruling *millet*, the Muslim *millet*, but, in fact, the Muslim populations of the Ottoman Empire were rent by major differences. One of these was the cleavage between the Sunni population and the Shii groups in the Empire. Shiism was a form of Islam that had been made into a state religion by the Persian dynasty which had been a rival of the Ottoman dynasty. Shii subjects of the Empire thus concealed their true religious allegiance and were considered as a sort of religious fifth column by the

Sunni Muslims (Martin, 1972:279). In theory, however, Shiis were simply a temporary aberration, an "exception to the rule". But there were other, possibly more important, lines of demarcation between various Islamic groups. During the First World War, an Ottoman intellectual who was serving in the Ottoman Army, found to his dismay that recruits who were nominally Muslims did not see themselves as Muslims, but would give him names of obscure local sects when it came to identifying their religious affiliation. This was their own focus of identity. This sectarian, provincial, "savage" i.e. peripheral Islam, made up a dimension of Ottoman society which the official, orthodox state-supported Islam combatted with determination but with little success. In this perspective, then, to think of Islam as covering and providing for the undivided allegiance of Muslim Ottomans was more of an ideological scheme intended to foster feelings of allegiance to the Centre than it was a social reality. We may say that there existed a "mythical" as well as "classificatory" aspect of Ottoman elite political culture.

## Military Culture

Another component and underpinning of the Ottoman state was military culture. Paul Wittek was the first to underline that the early forays of Ottoman princelings in Anatolia against the Byzantine frontier had succeeded because they were carried out by a special type of religio-military organization (Wittek, 1938). According to him, Ottoman warriors banded into groups guided by a code, that of "fighters for the faith" which legitimized their raids and provided a rationale for expansion. He called this the *Gazi* spirit (from *Gaza*, war carried out for Islam). Later research has attempted to debunk this theory and has given greater weight to the internal dynamics of the Turkmen groups which made up the Gazi forces. But there is no doubt that Wittek was on an important and fruitful track, even though the spirit of religious chivalry which he imputed to the Ottomans may have been less pervasive and conscious than he thought. There is no doubt that fighting, going to war, being trained as warriors continued for centuries to be a central feature of the organization of the Empire. Theoretically, all Ottoman Muslims were involved in this constant readiness for war, and this long before the *levée en masse*.

The best way to approach this feature of Ottoman society is to remember that what may be called the "military spirit" of the

Ottomans was not just simply a feature of the "superstructure" and that it was overdetermined by other "infrastructural" aspects of society. It is only by reconstructing the way in which rewards were distributed, power was enforced and socialization proceeded that we can recapture this convergence of various social processes in Ottoman society.

We may begin with economic organization. The economic structure of the Turkish village was one focussed on the need to draw out of villages the warriors needed for military campaigns. The "surplus" generated at this level was funnelled into the activities of the military machine. Not so long ago, a Turkish Pan-Turanian of early vintage who thereafter opted for Marxism describes how, at the time of the Balkan Wars (1912–13), villagers needed a simple cue to fall into a mobilization pattern. All that was required was for the news of mobilization to be heard.

> Shortly after the lithographic print which reproduced the mobilization order was hung on the wall of the Mosque, the Mosque square filled with peasants. When the peasants were all accounted for, the *imam* turned the palms of his hands upwards [as is done when a prayer is said]. First, he read a prayer for success in conquest. The prayer was having a strange, enveloping effect on the atmosphere of the square. When I cupped my hands I was overwhelmed by the feelings that the prayer had awakened in my soul. It was as if I was observing a swift change in me. There was something very effective and imagination-expanding in this prayer. For in "conquest" there lies an action, a heroic deed. This state, for centuries had lived an "era of conquests". (Aydemir, 1967:61).

From the village square, recruits set upon a path that had been used for centuries to gather men going on campaign. This brought them to a large meadow on which men of several villages were converging, and from there on they went to larger and larger gathering sites like the swelling of a river fed by rivulets. Even in those years the young man had been prepared for this great day by a socialization in which the exploits of heroes occupied an important place.

The policies of the Ottoman "centre" underline this involvement in military affairs. It is the *military* reverses of the Ottoman Empire which alerted its officials to the necessity for military and governmental reforms (Mardin, 1962;135). It is in the *military* institutions established by the Ottoman government that Western science and technology was first studied systematically (1792). The same is true of Western parliamentary democratic theories and of patriotism as a new ideology. Although these ideas first emerged among the civilian bureaucracy in the 1870s, it is the graduates of the military medical school of the 1890s, the Young Turks, who brought them to fruition. It is they who forced the Sultan to re-establish in 1908 the short-lived Ottoman Constitution of 1876 and who set out on the first, hesitant, programme of radical reforms in secularization and mobilized social energies for national defence. It is no coincidence that Mustafa Kemal (Atatürk), the founding father of the Turkish Republic, was both trained at the military academy and exposed to Young turk theories in his years of apprenticeship.

The Turkish Republic was founded in the wake of years of war in Anatolia against Greek occupying forces. It was the military success of Mustafa Kemal which produced the prestige which, subsequently, allowed him to abolish the Sultanate and the Caliphate. When the Turkish Grand National Assembly bestowed on him the title of *Gazi* following his victories, it did not realize that this *Gazi* was about to engage in moves which would radically secularize Turkish society, but it took a *Gazi* to undo the work of earlier *Gazis*. The military "spirit" and ideology, then, may be counted as one of the important value clusters which held the Empire together. It seems to have the energizing force for the Turkish-speaking ruling elite in the Empire.

## Religion

It has already become clear that military culture was a religio-military culture. Religion was also involved independently in the elaboration of an Ottoman "centre". There were, again, a number of levels at which religion was effective: Islam — as we have seen — was an ideological complex which aimed at uniting Muslims, and establishing a common frame of reference for the fragmented pieces of the Muslim population of the Empire. Education, which was controlled by religious personnel, linked the units of the "periphery" to the "centre" (Gibb and Bowen, 1957, 70 ff). So did the judiciary. The Muslim religious orders which gathered within their fold many of the inhabitants of the Empire were another Islamic frame under which persons with different "class" affiliations in a community could gather and coalesce. The religious orders, however, were only one in a variety of "corporate" groups such as guilds or brotherhoods, which enabled cross-linkages between the Muslim units and in some cases between the Muslim and the non-Muslim units (Gibbs and Bowen, 1957, 184, 192).

## Characteristics of the Ottoman State as Compared to the Western Nation-State

Although the machinery of the centre and the ideology that under-pinned it can be rendered with the Western concept of a "state", in fact, the Ottoman state did not have the same structural scaffolding as the Western nation-state. The Western nation-state was connected to its own periphery not by a series of vertical lines running from the centre to each community, but by a much richer and more elaborate network of "horizontal" lines. In this pattern town was linked to town, and province to province by an expanding market economy, by associations and firms. In addition, intermediate, quasi-representative bodies which originated in the periphery interposed themselves between the centre and the periphery. In France, in the late eighteenth century, a typical institutions of provincial scope of this sort would have been the provincial parliaments, staffed to a large extent by a specialized peripheral stratum, that of the *Noblesse de Robe*. Behind this growth of institutions of the periphery stood both the growth of towns and that of the bourgeoisie, and also the linkages the Monarchy had established with these relatively autonomous towns. Underlying this entire system was the idea of the legitimacy of associations with corporate personality before the law, which was absent in the Ottoman synthesis.

The idea of "horizontal network" may be clarified by a comparison of Ottoman and Austrian provincial organization. In the 1790s one province of Austria, Styria, "organized the military establishments on the Turkish border, provided chemists and midwives and other medical services, ran the customs, maintained the forests, appointed university professors" (Williams, 1970:10). There was no Ottoman equivalent of this powerful provincial organizational structure. In short, the Ottoman Empire had not gone through a "mercantilist" experience of the Western type or a "cameralist" phase, both of which had contributed to building local networks and linking them with the state. The Ottomans were good social engineers but the social structure which they worked with differed from that of the post-medieval West. These two societies were based on dissimilar structuring principles and actors within each one were forced into different sets of strategies.

## Ottoman Statesmen

The lynchpin of the Ottoman political system was the Ottoman official. Officials saw themselves as an elite of city dwellers (*sehrî*) and they looked upon the majority of the provincial and rural populations, including their own Muslim brothers, as backward clods. Rural Turks were included in this category even though Turkish, the language of only part of the population, was the language of state transactions. The term "Turk" was used by the official class as the equivalent of "hewers of wood and drawers of water" or as a synonym for "nomad". The elite considered itself to have transcended these origins of their putative ancestors who had migrated from Central Asia as a group of Turkmen nomads.

Ottoman officials saw themselves as guardians of a "state" and enforcers of a "reason of state" (*Devlet* and *Siyaset*). There also was a theory concerning the nature of the *devlet*: it had prospered as long as the equipoise of Ottoman social "orders" had been maintained (Mardin 1962). These "orders" consisted — in manuals which did not believe in long-winded statements — in the military (the name given to all officials), in tradesmen and husbandmen. As long as no one of these functional components had requested more than their "just share" the Ottoman Empire had risen. According to Ottoman observers of Ottoman decline who themselves originated in officialdom, Ottoman decline was due to a break in this equilibrium.

But the equipoise of these orders was a fiction in two respects. First, it is doubtful that these "orders" were able to articulate their demands efficiently. Secondly, one cannot recall a period in Ottoman history when the Empire was not threatened by some group or other "rocking the boat". In fact, historical sources provide us with a much more complex picture of social interaction and change in the Ottoman Empire. In this picture is figured a provincial gentry trying to cut loose from the surveillance of the Centre, turbulent tribes causing trouble in mountainous regions, insubordinate Janissaries wreaking havoc in anticipation of pay day, charismatic leaders challenging the authority of the state, and city mobs set in motion by one set of the elite against another set of the elite. Not only did not the official theory shun this information, it dismissed it as "exceptions" to the rule. The equilibrium model of society, reinforced at a number of levels, thus became a model of society in which Ottoman statesmen had a heavy political investment. Of course, the fact that the so called "military", the Ottoman patrimonial bureaucratic elite, had the lion's share of spoils, was also concealed.

Ottoman statesmen, then, worked with a picture of reality in which the acceptance of social segmentation was tantamount to treason, even though, in practice, these were the structures that statesmen had to manipulate. Thus the fundamentalist reformer Ibn Abd al-Wahhab, who was accepted in the Arab world by the end of the nineteenth century as an important reformer, was dismissed in the contemporary "History" of Cevdet Paşa, as nothing but a brigand (Cevdet, 1974; 167-172). Ottoman statesmen were, by and large, more "secular" than one could surmise from the title of Caliph held by the Sultan. In particular, they saw many of the fundamentalist currents originating in the provinces and in Anatolia as another threat to the equipoise of society. They looked at these currents as the works of dangerous fanatics unrepresentative of "real" Islam.

The difficulties encountered by the Ottoman statesmen in trying to build a nation-state show that their denial both of conflict as a significant datum of social life and their denial of legitimacy to "real" groups generated stumbling blocks that were difficult to overcome.

In the nineteenth century, modernist statesmen in the Ottoman Empire devised a system whereby the Muslim population nominally lost its position of superordination and began to be counted as just one more community in an empire which was made of religious communities. The Empire was now to function as a multicommunity system with members of all communities possessing equal rights before the law. This ingenious system — an ideal more than a reality — was a non-starter, since various non-Muslim communities within the Ottoman Empire refused to live as Ottomans: they became carriers of nationalism. Nationalism in some cases even transformed traditional communities into smaller units floated their own nationalism. Thus from the Greek Orthodox Church emerged the states of Greece, Serbia, Bulgaria and Rumania. Muslims followed suit. Albania and then the Arab-speaking provinces of the Ottoman Empire opted out. After many hesitations as to whether to use Islam as a principle of cohesion, Turkish nationalism was the idea around which the Turkish Republic was formed in 1923.

Turkish nationalism was therefore something of a new world-view for the Turks, even though the population inhabiting Anatolia, which constituted almost all of the territory of the Republic, was over-whelmingly Muslim. The founders of the Turkish Republic knew from their experience that this unity still concealed many real differences, but the official attitude was to conceal them. One of the reasons for which they insisted on the rule of a single party in Turkey was their apprehension that party politics would take advantage of these "natural" cleavages. At the same time they were convinced that "modernization", the establishment of a prosperous country linked by its stake in a market economy, would eliminate the old cleavages. They were also extremely careful — to the extent that their political vision and their means allowed — to preclude the rise of new social cleavages and, in particular, the creation of a "rootless" proletariat.

## *Modernization*

Of the devices successfully used by the Ottomans to build a policy for the Ottoman state during Ottoman expansion, the concept of *millet* had to be abandoned following the demise of the Empire. What was needed was to marshall the energies of a new nation. However, even after the instauration of the Turkish Republic (1923) suspiciousness with regard to "divisive" activities held fast. This is a term which one encounters whenever a crisis looms on the horizon in the Republic and its use continues in contemporary accounts of Turkish difficulties with its minorities. The Turkish Republic was "one and indivisible" but the threat to its unity did not come from *émigré* aristocrats: it originated in local social segments. This type of thinking was not entirely wrong: the large majority of Turks continued to live within social frameworks that had not been devised for a unitary nation and they received their sense of identity and purpose from smaller, local units which may be called communautarian. This was particularly true of underdeveloped Eastern Turkey but was not limited to it. Kurds were ruled by their traditional notables and saintly families and it was through those that they were in contact with the nation-state. Konya can be given as one example of a town where a local Dervish order still exerted very strong influence. Nakshibendi religious leaders led anti-Republican currents with surprising determination (and staying power) considering that they had been declared not to exist in 1925. Only among a small minority of persons educated in the higher schools of the Republic and republican *lycées* did new foci of *socialization* take hold. The Republic *did* have the political *allegiance* of a majority of the population. The mistake made by the Republicans was to assume that the diffuse social theory of the centre would automatically become the ideology of the periphery in the new conditions posited by the nation-state without an immense effort of education and social–structural change.

The Republic did attempt to replace the old Ottoman pluralism by a new pluralism of professional groups. The theory behind this idea was taken from Leon Bourgeois' solidarism and Durkheim's ideas concerning the division of labour. (Toprak, 1973). In fact, it was a restatement of the old theory of equipoise. Ottoman state theory had thus, phoenix-like, fastened on one of the more conservative social theories of modern Europe. What we know today is that at that particular time, the identity focus provided by membership in a labour organization or a teacher's union was unable to erase more primordial allegiances. Only much later were the former to be activated. Since there exists as yet no study of the interaction between the old and the new pluralism we cannot say much about the way in which these two divergent bases for group formation affected Turkey between 1930 and 1950. What we know is that the bureaucratic group which had assumed the function of the founding fathers of the Turkish Republic consisted of two types of personalities: those who were attuned to rumblings which were now originating in the periphery and those who were deaf to them. The first group was surprised to find out that despite the "modernization" of Turkey during the rule of the single party between 1923 and 1950 peripheral forces had been waiting for an opportunity to make an appearance. Among these, the force of religion caused the real surprise. This was not because religion as a force had been minimized. It was more because the religion that was seen to emerge was much more the "peripheral" islam of which the Ottomans had been so wary. This is probably an essential aspect of the religious revival of Turkey and has not been stressed in studies of Turkish Islam.

The party of the Founding Fathers, the Republican People's Party, lost the election of 1950 to an alliance of provincial notables and peasant leaders. The victorious Party, the Demokrat Party, had campaigned on an issue which consisted of a challenge to the military-bureaucratic policies of the Republican People's Party. It is true that the Demokrat Party had run on a platform of economic liberalization opposed to the policies of *étatisme* of the Republican People's Party. The Demokrat Party was spearheaded by large land-holders and persons dissatisfied with the economic policy of the Republican People's Party. But the label of "Party of the Peripheral Notables" fits the Demokrat party better than that of "Party of Capitalist and Allied Interests". In the end, it was another confrontation, that between secularism and Islam which gave the Demokrat Party its most wide-spread support is the countryside. This confrontation was simply a modification of the Ottoman confrontation between "official" and "peripheral" Islam. In "round one", the periphery had emerged as an alliance of the two sub-peripheral groups: the notables and localistic, Anatolian Islam.

The most interesting development, following the victory of the Demokrats, however, was that they too became aware of the currents which they had set in motion in the periphery and reacted by passing laws that preserved some of the foundations of the secular Republic and that proscribed the "exploitation" of religion.

## *"Demokratization"*

After 1950, with the democratization of Turkish politics a process began which has continued to the present. The bureaucratic elite of Turkey lost its grip on power with the entrance into politics of an increasing number of important, and later smaller, notables. Politics overwhelmed administration. The provincial governor was subordinated to the parliamentary representative. In addition, the private sector was given a new lease of life after 1950. This created a new monetary reward structure, which meant a loss of real income for bureaucrats as compared to a new class of entrepreneurs. The loss of income compounded the bureaucrat's loss of status. The bureaucrats, however, were just as derouted by the fact that the new developments did not fit their map of reality as by the decline of their position in society. It became a necessity to turn back the errors of the Demokrats which were subverting democracy. This thesis was not entirely false but it concealed a good dose of ideological confusion resulting from the perpetuation of old — Ottoman — values as to what constituted subversion. In this case subversion was defined in a manner not common to the idiom of democracy; it was identified with the weakening of the apparatus of state.

*Devlet* was able to hit back in 1960. At this time the Turkish military carried out a coup in the wake of which the leader of the Demokrat Party, Prime Minister Adnan Menderes, was executed. Round two was thus a victory for the forces of the Centre. But in this case, as in later interventions of the Turkish Army into the regime, one thing became clear: in the long run it was seen that the "military spirit" of old, despite the years under the Republic, was fired by fundamentally the same type of ideological steam as had propelled the Ottoman military. This paucity of theoretical thinking could not be attributed to the founder of the Republic: Atatürk had clearly seen the difference between military thinking and a civilian, industrial society. But the intervening military were not aware of these limitations.

In each one of these phases of the dialectical movement the consequences of political changes had been unanticipated: the first phase had introduced into politics an alliance that was not predicted, the second phase brought to the fore the resurgence of the military as guardians of the institutions of the Republic. What may be described as the third phase of Turkish politics since 1950 also had surprises in store for all concerned. This phase has been one in which the alliance of "peripheral" forces lost momentum and the component micro-social groups of the periphery began to assume greater importance. A similar segmentation appears in the forces representing the "Centre". All of this was happening at a time when the industrial structure of Turkey was finally beginning to emerge. Similarly, student radicalism surfaced at this time with a completely new force.

The 1960 military coup brought with it a new emphasis on egalitarianism by the rebellious officers. This new but diffuse ideological stance was what distinguished the "progressive" ideas of the 1960s from the earlier "populism" of the Republican People's Party. One way to conceptualize this change is to remember that even though the founders of the Republic had been of a similar background to the officers, they had still been able to see themselves as members of an Ottoman official elite. For reasons which are still obscure, the new group of 1960 saw itself much more as part of a "real" nation; possibly, the Republican emphasis on creating a "nation" had by now been crowned with success. The new classification had become meaningful for many Turks. Possibly, the fact that a "nation" was by now meaningful to Turks also set the concept of politics into a different conceptual frame despite the influence of Ottoman antecedents: in one camp were those who had the interests of the "nation" at heart, in the other those who were egotistically taking all for themselves. The similarities with the France of 1789–93 begin to appear here quite distinctly, and these attitudes were now much more marked than they were at the time of the Young Turks. But what made Turkey differ from France in 1789 was the much greater fragmentation of Turkey, which in the 1970s, became apparent, and which obscured relatively simple egalitarianism of the 1960s.

Among the students, similar self-placement into a national frame, together with the "de-elitization" of Turkish society, yielded socialism and anti-imperialism. Among a section of the working and the city "bidonville" classes, parallel trends were seen to develop. The Republican People's Party took advantage of this groundswell to change its ideology and bring it into line with these new currents. A new polarity for politics had thus emerged: the polarity between parties with a social-democratic ideology and those with a "capitalistic" ideology. But within it was still buried some of the old polarity between centre and periphery. In addition, a new type of peripheral phenomenon developed: the Shiites of Turkey became increasingly conscious of themselves as a group. They formed a political party which, though weak, is still in existence today. Kurdish intellectuals too began to voice demands for autonomy and independence. Thus the illusion that Turkey had once and for all become polarized within the common framework of a "nation" was, once more, dispelled. What has emerged from this new cross-cutting of cleavages and allegiances is a new Turkey: a Turkey partly fragmented along traditional lines and partly fragmented along modern lines. How and why the latest, ethnic and sub-religious, cleavages developed is still difficult to reconstruct, but the fact that Turkey is racked by a wave of social and political violence may be best explained by the fact that the old "central" ideological frame and the old social system have both been shattered. Now the time has come to develop a new *classification system* which will simultaneously have the function of a *political myth*. At least, it would seem that it was this combination which made the old system endure.

## Notes

(1) Shils' definition is as follows: "Society has a centre. There is a central zone in the structure of society. This central zone impinges in various ways on those who live within the ecological domain in which the society exists. Membership in the society, in more than the ecological sense of being located in a bounded territory and of adapting to an environment affected or made up by other persons located in the same territory, is constituted by relationships to this central zone.

The central zone is not, as such, a spatially located phenomenon. It almost always has a more or less definite location within the bounded territory in which the society lives. Its centrality has, however, nothing to do with geometry and little with geography.

The centre, or the central zone is a phenomenon of the realm of values and beliefs. It is the centre of the order of symbols, of values and beliefs, which govern the society. It is the centre because it is the ultimate and the irreducible; and it is felt to be such by many who cannot give explicit articulation of its irreducibility." (Shils, 1961:117)

Also for periphery: "As we move from the centre of society, the centre in which authority is possessed, to the hinterland or the periphery, over which authority is exercised, attachment to the central value system becomes attenuated." (Shils, 1961:124)

# References

Ahmet Cevdet (1271-1309 A.H.) (1974). *"Tarih"*, 12 Vols, Modern Turkish by Temelkuran, Istanbul.

Aydemir, S. S. (1967). "Suyu Arayan Adam", Remzi, Istanbul.

Eisenstadt, S. N. (1973). "Traditional Patrimonialism and Modern Neo-patrimonialism", Beverley Hills.

Gellner, E. (1969). The great patron: a reinterpretation of tribal rebellion, *Archives Européennes de Sociologie* **X**(1).

Gibb, H.A.R. and Bowen, Harold (1957). "Islamic Society and the West, A Study of the Impact of Western Civilization on Moslem Culture in the Near East", Vol. 1: "Islamic Society in the XVIIth Century", Part II, Royal Institute of International Affairs, Weidenfeld and Nicholson, London.

Gökalp, Z. (n.d.) "Türklesmek, Islâmlasmak, Muasírlasmak", Istanbul.

Inalcik, H. (1973). "The Ottoman Empire: The Classical Age 1300-1600", Trs. N. Itzkowitz and C. Imber, London.

Inalcik, H. (1977). Centralization and Decentralization in Ottoman Administration, *In* Studies in Eighteenth Century Islamic History (Eds Thomas Naff and Roger Owen), 27-52. Carbondale, Illinois.

Issawi, C. (1966). "The Economic History of the Middle East", University of Chicago Press, Chicago.

Landau, J. (1974). "Radical Politics in Modern Turkey", E. J. Brill, Leiden.

Mardin, S. (1962). "The Genesis of Young Ottoman Thought", Princeton University Press, Princeton.

Mardin, S. (1973). "Center-Periphery Relations: A Key to Turkish Politics?", *Daedalus* **102**, 169-190.

Martin, B. G. (1972). A Short History of the Khalwati Order of Dervishes, *In* "Scholars, Saints and Sufis", (Ed. N. Keddie), 275-306. University of California Press, Berkeley.

Meeker, M. E. (1972). The Great Family Aghas of Turkey — A Study of a Changing Political Culture. *In* "Rural Politics and Social Change in the Middle East", (Eds. R. Antoun and I. Harik), University of Indiana Press, Bloomington.

Mumcu, A. (1963). "Osmanli Devletinde Siyaseten Katl", Ajans Türk, Ankara.

Shils, E. (1961). Center and Periphery. *In* "The Logic of Personal Knowledge: Essays Presented to Michael Folanyi on his Seventieth Birthday, 11 March 1961", 117-130. The Free Press, Glencoe, Illinois.

Shaw, S. (1976). "History of the Ottoman Empire and Modern Turkey Volume I: Empire of the Gazis The Rise and the Decline of The Ottoman Empire 1280-1808", Cambridge University Press, Cambridge.

Sussnitzki, A. J. (1917). "Zur Gliederung Wirtschaftlicher Arbeit nach Nationalitäten in der Türkei", *Archiv fur Wirtschaftsforschung im Orient* **II**, 382-407, *In* "The Economic History of The Middle East", (Ed. C. Issawi), University of Chicago Press, Chicago. 1966, 27-52.

Toprak, Z. (1977). "2 Mesrutiyette solidarist düsünce: Halkciklik", *Toplum ve Bilim* I, 92-123.
Toynbee, A. (1951-1961). "A Study of History", Oxford University Press, London, 12 volumes.
Waterbury, J. (1970). "The Commander of the Faithful", Columbia University Press, New York.
Williams, E. N. (1970). "The Ancien Régime in Europe", Bodley Head, London and New York.
Wittek, P. (1938). "The Rise of the Ottoman Empire", Royal Asiatic Society Monographs, No. 23, London.

# Index